D1443893

AFRICAN NATIONS AND LEADERS

THE DIAGRAM GROUP

Facts On File, Inc.

History of Africa: African Nations and Leaders

Copyright © 2003 by The Diagram Group

Diagram Visual Information Ltd

Editorial director:	Denis Kennedy
Editor:	Peter Harrison
Contributor:	Keith Lye
Indexer:	Martin Hargreaves
Senior designer:	Lee Lawrence
Designers:	Claire Bojczuk, Christian Owens
Illustrators:	Kathy McDougall, Graham Rosewarne
Research:	Neil McKenna, Patricia Robertson

Facts On File, Inc.
132 West 31st Street
New York NY 10001

Library of Congress Cataloging-in-Publication Data
African nations and leaders / The Diagram Group.
    p. cm. – (History of Africa)
  Includes bibliographical references and index.
  ISBN 0-8160-5060-0 (set) – ISBN 0-8160-5066-X
   1. Africa–History–Miscellanea. I. Diagram Group. II. Series.

DT21 .A34 2003
960'.03–dc21   2002035201

Facts On File books are available at special discounts when purchased in bulk quantities for businesses, associations, institutions, or sales promotions. Please call our Special Sales Department in New York at 212/967-8800 or 800/322-8755.

You can find Facts On File on the World Wide Web at: http://www.factsonfile.com

Printed in the United States of America

EB DIAG 10 9 8 7 6 5 4 3 2 1

ntents

reword | 4–5

ATION STATES | 6–99

geria	6–7	Lesotho	52–53
gola	8–9	Liberia	54–55
nin	10–11	Libya	56–57
tswana	12–13	Malawi	58–59
rkina Faso	14–15	Mali	60–61
rundi	16–17	Mauritania	62–63
meroon	18–19	Morocco	64–65
ntral African Republic	20–21	Mozambique	66–67
ad	22–23	Namibia	68–69
ngo, Democratic		Niger	70–71
Republic of	24–25	Nigeria	72–73
ngo, Republic of	26–27	Rwanda	74–75
ibouti	28–29	Senegal	76–77
ypt	30–31	Sierra Leone	78–79
quatorial Guinea	32–33	Somalia	80–81
itrea	34–35	South Africa	82–83
hiopia	36–37	Sudan	84–85
bon	38–39	Swaziland	86–87
e Gambia	40–41	Tanzania	88–89
ana	42–43	Togo	90–91
inea	44–45	Tunisia	92–93
inea-Bissau	46–47	Uganda	94–95
ory Coast	48–49	Zambia	96–97
nya	50–51	Zimbabwe	98–99

LAND STATES | 100–106

pe Verde	100	Mauritius	104
moros	101	São Tomé and Príncipe	105
adagascar	102–103	Seychelles	106

bliography	107–108
dex	109–112

FOREWORD

The six-volume History of Africa series has been designed as a companion set to the Peoples of Africa series. Although, of necessity, there is some overlap between the two series, there is also a significan shift in focus. Whereas Peoples of Africa focuses on ethnographic issu that is the the individual human societies which make up the continen History of Africa graphically presents a historical overview of the political forces that shaped the vast continent today.

African Nations and Leaders focuses on the nation states of the continent of Africa, from Algeria to Zimbabwe. Following this A–Z listing appear the island states of Cape Verde, Comoros, Madagasca Mauritius, São Tomé and Príncipe, and the Seychelles. When used conjunction with the regional volumes in this series, *African Natior and Leaders* provides an invaluable overview of the whole of contemporary Africa from the time when the states first gained independence until the present day.

Inside this volume the reader will find, for each nation and island state, a textual analysis of their history since independence. This provides a summary of their struggle to achieve self-determination, the major influences for change, and their stability since achieving control over their own affairs.

There are also short biographies of the most significant leaders of these nation and island states. These provide a concise portrait of th leaders, many of whom provided the inspiration for change, and ga their people the confidence to believe in their own abilities and potential for success.

A timeline of the most important events in each nation states' histor provides an overview of its development from the most significant dates in its early history through to the current events, or personaliti which are shaping its future.

Taken as a whole, *African Nations and Leaders* gives the reader an insight into the struggles for independence, and the frequent difficulties experienced in maintaining stability after independence, the 53 independent nations. It also places them firmly within their historical context, and highlights the major personalities who have done much to influence their destinies.

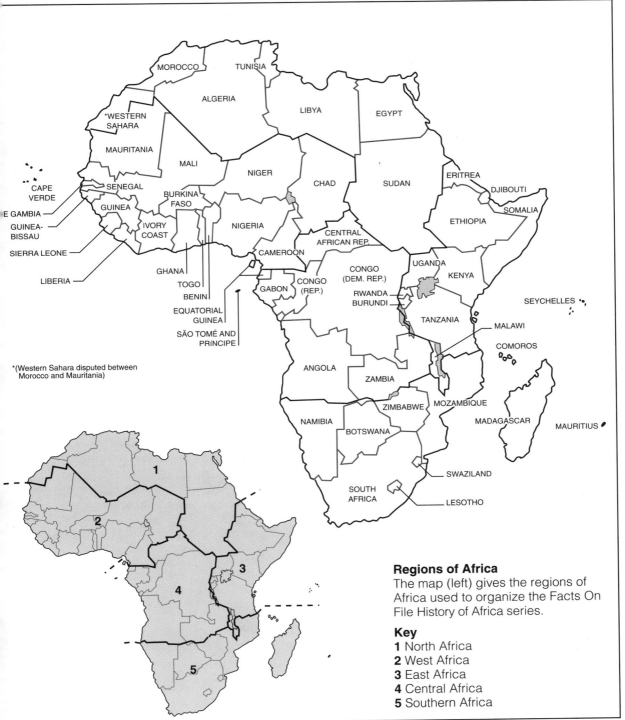

MOROCCO TUNISIA

ALGERIA LIBYA EGYPT

*WESTERN SAHARA

MAURITANIA MALI NIGER CHAD SUDAN ERITREA

DJIBOUTI

CAPE VERDE SENEGAL BURKINA FASO SOMALIA

E GAMBIA GUINEA ETHIOPIA

GUINEA-BISSAU IVORY COAST NIGERIA CENTRAL AFRICAN REP.

SIERRA LEONE CAMEROON UGANDA KENYA

GHANA CONGO (DEM. REP.)

LIBERIA TOGO GABON CONGO (REP.) RWANDA SEYCHELLES

BENIN BURUNDI

EQUATORIAL GUINEA TANZANIA MALAWI

SÃO TOMÉ AND PRÍNCIPE COMOROS

*(Western Sahara disputed between Morocco and Mauritania) ANGOLA ZAMBIA MADAGASCAR

MAURITIUS

NAMIBIA ZIMBABWE MOZAMBIQUE

BOTSWANA

SWAZILAND

SOUTH AFRICA LESOTHO

Regions of Africa
The map (left) gives the regions of Africa used to organize the Facts On File History of Africa series.

Key
1 North Africa
2 West Africa
3 East Africa
4 Central Africa
5 Southern Africa

Algeria

Many Europeans settled in Algeria when it was a French colony, but most Algerian people disliked French rule. In 1954, Algerian Muslims formed the National Liberation Front (FLN), which started a revolutio. After a bitter civil war, Algeria won its independence on July 3, 1962. Most Europeans then left Algeria. In 1963, Muhammad Ahmad Ben Bella, the country's prime minister and FLN leader, was elected president. He declared Algeria a socialist state and made the FLN the only political party. Alarmed at Ben Bella's actions, army officers deposed him in June 1965. A mainly military government under Color Houari Boumédienne was set up. In 1976, Boumédienne was elected president and, in 1977, a National Assembly was elected. Only memb of the FLN were allowed to stand.

Boumédienne died in 1978 and was succeeded by Chadli Bendjedid. 1980, many Berbers, who form a minority in Algeria, rioted when Cha announced that Arabic would become the only official language. In 1989, Benjedid introduced a multiparty system. In elections in 1991, tl *Institut Islamique du Salut* (Islamic Salvation Front, or FIS) won a majority of seats in parliament. But the FLN government stopped the FIS, which consisted of anti-Western Islamic fundamentalists, from taking power. Bendjedid resigned in 1992 and a new military regime banned the FIS. Civil war broke out and about 100,000 were killed in 1990s. Elections were held in 1999, but political parties based on religi were banned. Abdelaziz Bouteflika, who was elected president, worke to restore peace. His policies reduced the bloodshed. Peace returned to the cities and towns, though fighting continued in rural areas. In 2001, Bouteflika announced that Berber would become a national language.

A colonial legacy
French soldiers opposed Algerian Muslims during the civil war in the 1950s.

Muslims at prayer
Radical Islamic, Algerian groups gained support during the 1990s.

Leaders

Ben Bella, Muhammad Ahmad
(1916–)
A leader in the struggle for Algeria's independence, Ben Bella was imprisoned twice by the French, first in 1950–1952 and again in 1956–1962. He became prime minister in 1962 and was elected president in 1963. But he ruled in a dictatorial way and was overthrown in a coup in 1965. He was placed under house arrest until 1979.

Boumédienne, Houari
(1925–1978)
A former guerrilla fighter against the French during the struggle for independence, Boumédienne became president of Algeria in July 1965, following a bloodless coup which overthrew Ben Bella. In 1967 he survived an attempted coup and, as president, followed socialist policies and ended Algeria's special relationship with France.

Bouteflika, Abdelaziz
(1937–)
Born in Morocco of Algerian parents, Bouteflika served in the FLN during Algeria's struggle for independence. He was elected president in 1999 after the other six presidential candidates withdrew, alleging that he was the preferred candidate of the army. In office, his priority was to bring peace to his divided country.

…erian timeline

c. 3000 BCE	Berbers migrate to the Algeria region
c. 1000 BCE	Phoenicians create colonies on the Algerian coast
c. 200 BCE	Massinissa establishes the kingdom of Numidia in northern Algeria
44 CE	Numidia is formally annexed by the Roman Empire
432	The Vandals settle on the coast of Algeria
682–702	Muslim Arab conquest of Algeria
1518	The Turkish pirate Barbarossa captures Algiers for the Ottoman Empire

The Medracen
This second-century Numidian royal tomb was built in what is now the eastern part of Algeria.

…h century

1815	US navy attacks bases of the Barbary Corsairs in Algiers
1830	The French capture Algiers
1848	Algeria is declared an integral part of France
1902	Algeria's present boundaries established
1943	Ferhat Abbas calls for Algerian independence
1944	French citizenship granted to many Algerians
1947	Algerian Muslims are given limited voting rights
1954	National Liberation Front (FLN) begins war of independence against France
1956–1957	France defeats the FLN in the Battle of Algiers
1958	French army rebels and French settlers seize control of the colonial government in Algeria
1959	President de Gaulle of France decides to offer Algeria self-determination
1960	Rebellion of French settlers suppressed
1962 July 3	Algeria becomes independent of France
1965	Military coup overthrows Ben Bella; Boumédienne becomes president
1979	Chadli Bendjedid of the FLN becomes president after an election in which he is the only candidate
1989	Algeria, Morocco and Tunisia form the Arab Maghrib Union
1990	Fundamentalist Islamic Salvation Front (FIS) enjoys unexpected success in local government elections
1991	After the FIS wins first round in general elections, the government declares a state of emergency
1992	President Bendjedid resigns, a military regime is established and Islamic fundamentalists begin a terrorist campaign
1995	Liamine Zeroual is appointed president
1996	Algerians approve a new constitution banning political parties based on religion, sex or language
1999	President Zeroual resigns and Abdelaziz Bouteflika is elected president
2000	Under an amnesty, large numbers of Islamic militants hand over their arms
2001	Riots occur among Berbers
2002	Government wins absolute majority in elections

Constitution
This stamp, issued in 1963, celebrated the proclamation of the Algerian constitution.

Internal conflict
Pro-government troops battled with Muslim fundamentalists in Algeria in 1991.

© DIAGRAM

7

Angola

From the 17th century, the Portuguese held control over the Angolan coast and, by 1921, they ruled the entire territory. In 1951, Angola became an Overseas Province of Portugal. But African opposition to Portuguese rule was increasing. In 1961, the Popular Movement for the Independence of Angola (MPLA), which had been formed in 1956, staged a revolt in Luanda. The MPLA was one of three groups opposed to Portuguese rule. In the north, the chief group was Holden Roberto's Front for the Liberation of Angola (FNLA). The main group in the south was Jonas Savimbi's National Union for the Total Liberation of Angola (UNITA). In April 1974, a coup in Portugal brought a military regime to power, which agreed to independence for Angola in November, 1975.

MPLA triumph
This stamp was issued to promote victory for the Popular Movement for the Independence of Angola (MPLA).

The Marxist-Leninist (Communist) MPLA formed the government and Dr Antoniu Agostinho Neto became the first president. However, the civil war continued as the three main groups fought for power. By April 1976, the MPLA government held control of 12 of Angola's 15 provinces. But the UNITA rebels in the south continued the war, receiving aid from the West, notably South Africa and the US. The western-backed FNLA also carried out guerrilla warfare in the north, but it became inactive after 1984. A peace accord was signed in May 1991. In multiparty elections held in 1992, the MPLA, which had renounced Marxist-Leninist policies, won a majority, and José Eduardo dos Santos was reelected president. But UNITA refused to accept the result and the civil war resumed in 1994. A coalition government was formed in 1997 but Jonas Savimbi refused to join it. Full-scale civil war resumed in 1999. However, after Jonas Savimbi was killed in action in February 2002, UNITA agreed to a ceasefire which was signed in April 2002.

Heroes of communism
Marx, Engels and Lenin are glorified by the MPLA on this street poster in the 1960s.

Leaders

dos Santos, José Eduardo
(1942–)
Dos Santos became president of Angola on the death of Antoniu Agostinho Neto in 1979. He was reelected in 1985 and 1992. In 1994–1995, he negotiated a ceasefire with the South African-backed UNITA guerrillas, but the UNITA leader Jonas Savimbi refused to take up the post of vice-president and the civil war restarted.

Neto, Dr Antoniu Agostinho
(1922–1979)
A poet and Marxist politician, Neto became the first president of Angola in 1974. He served until his death in 1979. He had earlier led the MPLA forces against the Portuguese colonial regime. His period in office was marked by conflict as government forces fought to put down the rival FNLA in the north and UNITA in the south.

Savimbi, Jonas Malheiro
(1934–2002)
An opponent of Portuguese colonialism, Jonas Savimbi first worked with the FLNA, but, in 1966, he set up UNITA. He led UNITA in the struggle against Portuguese rule. After independence in 1975, he led UNITA in a guerrilla war against the Angolan government. He was killed in action in February 2002.

gola timeline

-19th century

1483 CE	Portuguese explorers reach Angola
1490	Portuguese convert King Nzinga Nkuwu of Kongo (in northern Angola) to Christianity
1575	The Portuguese found Luanda as a base for slaving operations
1623–1626	Queen Nzinga of Ndongo in present-day Angola is defeated in a war against Portuguese slave traders
1641	The Dutch drive the Portuguese out of Angola
1648	The Portuguese regain control of Angola from the Dutch

h century

1884	The Portuguese begin to extend their control inland from the coast
1921	Portugal gains full control of all of modern Angola
1956	Pro-independence Popular Movement for the Liberation of Angola (MPLA) is formed
1961	An MPLA uprising in Luanda is defeated by the Portuguese
1962	Northern Angolan rebels organize the Front for the Liberation of Angola (FNLA)
1966	Southern Angolan rebels form the National Union for the Total Liberation of Angola (UNITA)
1974	Portugal announces its intention to withdraw from Angola. Civil war breaks out between MPLA, FNLA and UNITA. Cuban troops support MPLA, South Africans give aid to UNITA.
1975	**Nov. 11** Angola becomes independent of Portugal: MPLA unilaterally forms a government in Luanda
1976	The UN recognizes the MPLA as the legitimate government of Angola
1977	Attempted coup by dissidents within the MPLA
1981	South African forces advance 100 miles into Angola to support UNITA
1984	FNLA withdraws from military operations
1986	US begins to send aid to UNITA
1988	Cuba and South Africa agree to stop aiding the MPLA and UNITA
1989	MPLA and UNITA agree a ceasefire
1990	The MPLA renounces Marxism
1991	MPLA and UNITA agree a ceasefire
1992	The MPLA's José Eduardo dos Santos becomes president after multiparty elections. UNITA begins the civil war again
1994	New peace agreement signed by the MPLA and UNITA
1995	UN peacekeeping force oversees the peace agreement
1997	New government of national unity formed
1999	Civil war breaks out again between MPLA and UNITA
2000	UNITA launches new offensives, continuing the civil war
2002	Jonas Savimbi is killed in action and a ceasefire is agreed

Portuguese soldier
Portuguese control over the Angolan coast began in the 1600s.

MPLA soldier
The MPLA fought against UNITA and the FNLA in the Angolan civil war.

UNITA soldiers
This rebel movement was backed by the US and also South Africa.

© DIAGRAM

9

Benin

France annexed Dahomey (now Benin) in 1904 and made it part of its huge territory of French West Africa. In 1946, Dahomey became an overseas province of France, but opposition to French rule increased. The country became independent on August 1, 1960. Newly independ Dahomey suffered from political instability, caused mainly by politica and regional rivalries. The first president was Hubert Maga, but he wa overthrown in 1963 by an army coup led by General Christophe Soglo A three-man presidential council was set up in 1970, with Hubert Mag as the first head of state in a rotational system. This government was overthrown by a coup in 1972 and Lt.-Col. Mathieu (later Ahmed) Kérékou became head of state. Kérékou faced many economic proble internal conflict and frequent plots. In 1975, his government announce that Dahomey would be renamed the People's Republic of Benin, and would follow Marxist-Leninist (Communist) policies. The governmen took over some parts of the economy, but many private businesses wer allowed to continue. From 1977, the only party permitted was the Ben People's Revolutionary Party. It held power until 1989, when Kérékou announced that Marxist-Leninism had been abandoned.

In 1990, a civilian group restored democracy. It legalized all parties a appointed a former World Bank executive, Nicéphore Soglo, as the prime minister to serve until elections were held in 1991. In 1991, Sog was elected president, comfortably defeating Kérékou. However, Kérékou was reelected in 1966, returning to power as president. He formed a government of national unity, which tried to revive the weak national economy. In 2001, President Kérékou was reelected president defeating his old opponent Nicéphore Soglo.

Victims
Trees, bearing the corpses of sacrificial victims, were found by the British upon arrival in Benin City in 1897.

Leaders

Kérékou, Mathieu Ahmed
(1928–)
Mathieu Kérékou became president of Dahomey (now Benin) in 1972, following a coup. He adopted Marxist-Leninist policies, but his government abandoned its leftwing policies in 1989. Kérékou was defeated in multiparty elections in 1991, but regained power in 1996. He was reelected in 2001.

Maga, Hubert Coutoucou
(1924–)
Maga entered politics after World War II and served as a deputy in the French parliament (1951–1958). He became the first president of Dahomey (now Benin) in 1960, but was deposed in 1963. He returned to office between 1970 and 1972, but was again overthrown in a coup. He was under arrest between 1972 and 1981.

Soglo, Christophe
(1909–1984)
Soglo joined the French army in 1931 and distinguished himself World War II and later in Indochina. In 1960, he became military adviser to President Mag Soglo staged a coup in 1963 and became head of state until 1964. He again intervened in 1965 and was head of state until deposed by younger army officers in 1967.

Benin City c.1668
An imaginative view of the city shows the steady procession of the *Oba* (king), followed by musicians, jesters and leopards, and, finally, the army.

Wooden door
Animals and weapons adorn this relic from a royal palace in Abomey, the former capital city.

˙in timeline

˙-19th century	
1625 CE	King Dako of Abomey founds the kingdom of Dahomey in present-day Benin
˙h century	
1807	Britain outlaws the slave trade, causing an economic crisis in Dahomey
1851	France signs a trade agreement with Dahomey
˙0–1949	
1904	France annexes the kingdom of Dahomey and incorporates it into French West Africa
1946	Dahomey becomes an overseas territory of France
˙0–1959	
1958	Dahomey is granted self-government by France
˙0–1969	
1960	**Aug 1** Dahomey becomes a fully independent republic
1960–1972	Frequent changes of government due to military coups
˙0–1979	
1972	Lt. Col. Mathieu Kérékou becomes president after a military coup
1975	Dahomey is renamed Benin. Marxist-Leninism introduced
˙0–1989	
1989	Marxist-Leninist ideology abandoned
˙0–1999	
1990	Kérékou's government is dissolved and political parties are legalized
1991	Nicéphore Soglo becomes president after Benin's first multiparty elections
1996	Kérékou returns to power as a democratically-elected president
1997	Labor unions protest government's economic liberalization measures
˙0–	
2001	President Kérékou is reelected after two of the presidential candidates withdraw in the second round of voting

Oba **Ovonramwen**
A former king of Benin, he was exiled in 1897.

Under foreign control
Dahomey (now known as Benin) became an overseas province of France in 1946.

© DIAGRAM

Botswana

Britain set up the Protectorate (colony) of Bechuanaland (present-day Botswana) in 1885. The South African government wanted to take ove[r] Bechuanaland, together with Basutoland (now Lesotho) and Swazilan[d] But, in 1935, Britain declared that no transfer would take place unless people were consulted. In 1950, a crisis occurred in Bechuanaland whe[n] Chief Seretse Khama (later Sir Seretse Khama) married Ruth William[s] white woman, while he was in Britain. South Africa was angered because it had outlawed interracial marriages. Seretse was exiled, but [he] was allowed to return in 1956 as an ordinary citizen. He then became involved in politics. In the general election in 1965, the Bechuanaland (now Botswana) Democratic Party (BDP), led by Seretse Khama, won majority. The country became independent as the Republic of Botswan[a] on September 30, 1966 and Seretse Khama became president of a stab[le] multiparty democracy. Seretse Khama died in 1980. He was succeede[d] by Dr Ketumile Masire, who served as president until 1998 when he, i[n] turn, was succeeded by Festus Mogae.

At independence, the economy was based on the export of meat and live animals. But, by 1997, Botswana had become a major diamond producer. By 1999, diamond and other mining had helped Botswana t[o] increase its per capita GNP (gross national product) to US $3,240, one [of] Africa's highest rates. The country also set up animal reserves, thus encouraging tourism. But Botswana faces many problems, including unemployment, overgrazing, soil erosion, and the spread of AIDS, whi[ch] affects one in five of all adults in Botswana. A 1999 forecast predicted that children born in the early 2000s would have an average life expectancy of 40. Without AIDS, it would have been nearly 70.

A year to celebrate
The National Assembly building features on this stamp, issued in 1966, to mark Botswana's independence.

Leaders

Khama, Sir Seretse
(1921–1980)
Seretse Khama became the first prime minister of Botswana (Bechuanaland) in 1965 and served as president from its independence in 1966 until his death. He was exiled to Britain between 1950 and 1956 as a result of his marriage to a white British woman in 1948. To return, he renounced his position as chief.

Masire, Sir (Quett) Ketumile Joni
(1925–)
A founder of the ruling Botswana Democratic Party, Masire became vice-president of Botswana in 1966. In 1980, he became president, following the death of Seretse Khama. He was reelected in 1984, 1989 and 1994. He retired in 1988 and was succeeded by Festus Mogae. He maintained Botswana's stability.

Mogae, Festus
(1939–)
A former planning officer, financ[e] administrator and vice-presiden[t] of Botswana, Mogae was sworn [in] as president of Botswana in Apr[il] 1998. He succeeded Sir Ketumi[le] Masire, who had announced his impending retirement in 1997. Mogae chose Lieutenant-General Seretse Ian Khama, son of Seretse Khama, as his vice-president.

:swana timeline

	c. 420 CE	Earliest dated evidence of farming and ironworking in Botswana
	c. 1095	Tswana people migrate to the area of modern Botswana from the north
h century		
	1801	British missionaries visit the Tswana people
	1817	The London Missionary Society creates a permanent mission station at Kuruman
	1840s	David Livingstone active as a missionary in Botswana
	1860s	Tswana seek British protection against their enemies
	1867–1869	An influx of white prospectors follows the discovery of gold
	1885	With the agreement of King Khama III and other chiefs, Britain declares the Bechuanaland Protectorate
	1895	Tswana chiefs cede land to the British South Africa Company for railroad construction
)0–1949	**1935**	Britain rejects a request for Bechuanaland to be transferred to South African control
60–1959	**1950**	Chief Seretse Khama is refused permission to return to Botswana after he marries an Englishwoman
	1956	Seretse Khama given leave to return to Botswana
60–1969	**1960**	Bechuanaland is granted a legislative assembly
	1961	Seretse Khama forms the Bechuanaland (later Botswana) Democratic Party (BDP)
	1964	A new administrative capital is built at Gaborone
	1965	Britain grants Bechuanaland internal self-government
	1966	**Sept 30** Bechuanaland becomes independent as the republic of Botswana. Seretse Khama becomes the first president
	1967	Diamonds discovered at Orapa
	1969	The national assembly reelects Seretse Khama as president
70–1979	**1977**	The first all-weather road between Botswana and Zambia is completed
30–1989	**1980**	Seretse Khama dies, Dr Ketumile Masire succeeds as head of the BDP
	1982	Drought causes serious losses of livestock
	1984	The BDP wins the first elections after Khama's death
	1986	South African army raid on Gaborone
	1987	South Africa blockades the capital Gaborone
	1989	South African covert operations against African National Congress refugees cause tension
30–1999	**1990s**	Botswana becomes the second largest exporter of diamonds after Russia
	1998	Masire retires and Festus Mogae becomes president
	1999	BDP retains power in general elections
)0–	**2002**	The Baswara (San) people of the Central Kalahari Game Reserve protest against government attempts to evict them from their traditional lands

David Livingstone
Both explorer and missionary, he ecouraged the spread of Christianity, and the expansion of trade with Europe, in the hope that the slave trade would be brought to an end.

Dressed for battle
A Tswana warrior in typical costume, and bearing a distinctively-shaped shield, in the 19th century.

© DIAGRAM

Burkina Faso

French influence in Upper Volta (now Burkina Faso) began in the 188(
and, in 1919, it became a French colony. In 1932, France divided the
land between Ivory Coast, Niger and French Sudan (now Mali). But, ir
1947, France recreated Upper Volta, which became independent on
August 5, 1960. The first president was Maurice Yaméogo. His
government was inefficient and corrupt and many people disliked his
dictatorial rule. In 1966, the army removed Yaméogo from office.
General Sangoulé Lamizana took power, and became the leader of a
military government. In 1970, Lamizana turned over some power to th
prime minister though he remained president. In 1973, the military
resumed power over the country, whose economy had been badly hit b
inflation, while a drought had caused starvation in country areas.

Lamizana continued to serve as president and, in 1977, elections wer
held under a multiparty system. Lamizana was elected president in 197
but, in 1980, he was overthrown by Colonel Sayé Zerbo. Zerbo was
overthrown in 1982, and Major Jean-Baptiste Ouédraogo became
president. Ouédraogo's rule was shortlived. He was removed from offi
in a coup in 1983 and Captain Thomas Sankara, leader of a group of
radical young officers, seized power. Sankara and his allies formed a
National Revolutionary Council, and introduced radical policies. In
1984, the government announced that the country would be renamed
Burkina Faso, a name meaning "the land of honest men." Sankara
purged the civil service and military, and introduced national service, b
was assassinated in 1987. He was replaced by Captain Blaise Compao
who was elected president in 1991 and worked to stabilize the econom
In 1998, Compaoré was reelected president by a large majority.

Maurice Yaméogo
He was the first
president of Upper
Volta (now known as
Burkina Faso) from
1960–1966.

Leaders

Compaoré, Blaise
(1951–)
Compaoré became president of
Burkina Faso in 1987, following a
coup in which he deposed his
former friend Thomas Sankara. He
was reelected in 1991 and 1998.
Compaoré renounced Sankara's
socialist policies,
introducing a program
of privatization and
austerity supported by
the International
Monetary Fund.

Lamizana, Sangoulé
(1916–)
Lamizana became army chief of
staff of Upper Volta in 1961. In
1966, he led a coup to overthrow
Maurice Yaméogo. In 1970, while
president, he handed some power
to the prime minister but in 1973,
he took power again. He was
elected president in 1978, but, in
1980, he was overthrown by a
military coup led by Colonel Zerbo.

Sankara, Thomas
(1949–1987)
Sankara became prime minister
Upper Volta in 1982. In 1983, he
staged a coup and became
president. He introduced
development programs intended
to reform the economy and help
rural areas. He was
killed in 1987 in a coup
mounted by one of his
closest aides, Blaise
Compaoré, who had
become a rival.

rkina Faso timeline

e-19th century

c. 1300 CE	Mossi kingdom founded in the area of present-day Burkina Faso
c. 1450	Mossi establish a capital at Ouagadougou

th century

1896	France captures Ouagadougou
1897	The Mossi kingdom formally becomes a French protectorate

00–1949

1919	France creates the colony of Upper Volta within the borders of present-day Burkina Faso

50–1959

1958	France grants Upper Volta internal self-government

60–1979

1960	**Aug. 5** Upper Volta becomes independent: Maurice Yaméogo becomes president
1966	Yaméogo is overthrown by a military coup: Gen. Sangoulé Lamizana becomes president
1970	Lamizana gives executive powers to a civilian prime minister
1973	The prime minister is dismissed and Lamizana suspends the constitution. He continues as head of a military government
1978	Lamizana is elected president under a multiparty system

80–1989

1980	Lamizana is overthrown by a military coup
1983	Capt. Thomas Sankara becomes president: he changes the name of the country to Burkina Faso
1987	Sankara is assassinated during a military coup: Capt. Blaise Compaoré becomes president

90–1999

1997	Drought severely affects agriculture
1998	Compaoré is reelected president

00–

2001	A health crisis occurs when more than 1,500 people die in an outbreak of meningitis. Around seven percent of adults in Burkina Faso are reported to be infected with HIV

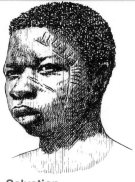

Salvation
This Mossi boy's face has been scarred to prevent his being taken as a slave.

Quezzin Coulibaly
He was president of Upper Volta between 1957–1958, before it became independent from France.

Mogho naba
He was the supreme ruler of the Mossi, and exercised his power from the court of Ouagadougou, the current capital of Burkina Faso.

© DIAGRAM

15

Burundi

The first people of Burundi were the Twa. During the first millennium, the ancestors of the modern Hutu reached the area. Then, around 600 years ago, the ancestors of the modern Tutsi people moved into the area. The Tutsi founded kingdoms, ruled by *mwamis* (kings). They treated the majority Hutu as slaves. In 1897, Germany made an area called Ruanda-Urundi part of German East Africa. After World War I, the League of Nations asked Belgium to rule the area. In 1961, the people of Urundi (now Burundi) voted to become a monarchy under *Mwami* Mwambutsa IV. Ruanda (now Rwanda) voted to become a republic. Both countries became independent on July 1, 1962.

In 1965, assassins killed the Tutsi prime minister, while, later that year, Hutu officers launched a coup, which was harshly repressed. In 1966, Mwambutsa's son proclaimed himself head of state as Ntare V. But the prime minister Michel Micombero deposed Ntare. He made Burundi a republic, making himself president. Between 1966 and 1972, most Hutu and some moderate Tutsi were removed from high office and the army. In 1972, some Hutu tried to overthrow the government. This rebellion led to between 100,000 and 200,000 deaths, most of whom were Hutu. In 1976, Colonel Jean-Baptiste Bagaza seized power. He brought in reforms, but army officers overthrew him in 1987. He was replaced by Major Pierre Buyoya. Another uprising occurred in 1988 when 5,000 or more people were killed. In 1993, Buyoya was defeated in elections by Melchior Ndadaye, but Ndadaye was killed in a coup. This led to more conflict. In 1996, Buyoya became president after another coup. In 2000, most Hutu and Tutsi parties signed an agreement aimed at ending the civil war.

Funeral in Burundi
In 1996 Hutu president Ntibantungana pays his respects after the massacre of 320 people at a refugee camp.

Leaders

Buyoya, Pierre
(1949–)
Pierre Buyoya was a Tutsi army officer who became president of Burundi in 1987. He was defeated in elections in 1993 by a Hutu named Melchior Ndadaye, who was assassinated later that year. Buyoya again became president in 1996. In the early 2000s, Buyoya worked to achieve a peace agreement.

Micombero, Michel
(1940–1983)
In 1966, Michel Micombero, the prime minister of Burundi, deposed the *mwami* (king) and made the country a republic. He declared himself president and purged the army and the government of Hutu. After a failed coup in 1972, more than 100,000 people were killed. He was deposed in 1976 and exiled.

Mwambutsa IV
(1912–1977)
Mwambutsa IV served as *mwami* (king) of Burundi from 1915 until 1966. In 1965, after he had conspired with a group of Tutsi officers in an unsuccessful coup, he fled the country and later died in exile. His son Ntare V was proclaimed *mwami* in 1966, but he was removed from office when Burundi became a republic.

rundi timeline

t millennium CE		The Hutu people settle in the Burundi region
14th century		The Tutsi invade Burundi and conquer the Hutu
th century	1897	Burundi becomes part of German East African territory of Ruanda-Urundi
00–1949	1916	Belgian troops occupy Ruanda-Urundi
	1920	The League of Nations awards Ruanda-Urundi to Belgium as a mandated territory
60–1969	1961	Urundi votes to separate from Ruanda-Urundi and become the independent kingdom of Burundi
	1962	**July 1** Burundi becomes independent
	1966	Burundi becomes a republic
70–1979	1972	An unsuccessful Hutu revolt results in about 100,000 deaths
90–1999	1994	Hutu-Tutsi massacres occur when a plane carrying newly-elected president Ntaryamira of Burundi and president Habyarimana of Rwanda is shot down over Rwanda
	1996	Burundi expels thousands of Rwandan Hutu refugees
00–	2000	Attempts to negotiate a peace treaty in Tanzania are thwarted by extremist groups
	2001	A peace agreement is signed by President Buyoya and most Hutu and Tutsi political parties. A provisional government, containing members of all groups, is set up

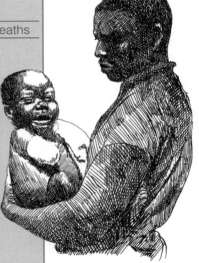

Innocent victim
The Tutsi retaliated with savagery after an abortive Hutu revolt in Burundi in 1972.

Colonial power
Ruanda-Urundi was part of the Belgian Congo until independence in 1962, when Ruanda became Rwanda and Urundi changed its name to Burundi.

King Mwambutsa IV
This 1962 stamp celebrated Burundi's independence.

© DIAGRAM

17

Cameroon

Union flag
A stamp, issued in 1962, which celebrated the first anniversary of the Union of African and Malagasy States.

Britain, France and Germany competed for control of the region which now makes up Cameroon in the late 19th century. In 1884, Germany made the region a protectorate (colony) called Kamerun. Allied troops invaded Kamerun during World War I. After the war, the League of Nations mandated Britain and France to rule the territory. British Cameroons consisted of two parts – Northern and Southern Cameroon. These areas were located along the Nigerian border. In 1946, French Cameroun and the British Cameroons became United Nations trust territories. French Cameroun became independent as the Republic of Cameroon on January 1, 1960 and Ahmadou Ahidjo became president. In February 1961, Northern Cameroons voted to unite with the Federation of Nigeria on June 1, 1961, while Southern Cameroons voted to join the Republic of Cameroon. Southern Cameroons then joined the Republic of Cameroon to form the Federal Republic of Cameroon. It consisted of two states – East and West Cameroon.

From 1966, the federal republic was ruled by a single party, the Cameroon National Union (CNU). In 1972, the country was renamed the United Republic of Cameroon and federal form of government was dropped. The country's name was changed to Republic of Cameroon in 1982, and Ahidjo resigned as president. His successor was Paul Biya. In 1985, Biya renamed his party the People's Democratic Movement. Opposition parties were legalized in 1991 and elections in 1992 and 1997 resulted in victory for Biya and his party. In the 1990s, Cameroon faced border disputes with Nigeria, especially over the oil-rich Bakassi peninsula. President Biya's 1997 re-election was boycotted by the major opposition parties. He can stand for another 7-year term in 2004.

Leaders

Ahidjo, Ahmadou
(1924–1989)
Ahmadou Ahidjo was prime minister of French Cameroun from 1958–1960. He then served as president from 1960–1982, when he resigned because of ill health. He remained leader of the ruling Cameroon National Union, but he clashed with the new president, Paul Biya. In 1983, he went into exile in France.

Biya, Paul
(1928–)
Biya served as prime minister between 1975–1982. In 1982, he became the country's second president following the resignation of President Ahidjo. He survived a coup attempt in 1984. Biya legalized opposition parties in 1991 and he was reelected president in multiparty elections in 1992 and 1997.

M'Bida, André-Marie
(1917–)
M'Bida who had served as a member of the French Assembly became prime minister of French Cameroun in 1957. However, he was accused of being too pro-French and his government was overthrown in 1958. Following a period in exile, he returned in 1960, and served as opposition leader.

meroon timeline

e-19th century

c. 200 CE Bantu-speaking peoples, modern Africa's largest linguistic group, originate in Cameroon and eastern Nigeria

1472 Portuguese navigator Fernãndo Po becomes the first European to visit Cameroon

h century

1884 Cameroon becomes a German protectorate

00–1949

1914 French and British troops occupy Cameroon

1922 Cameroon is divided between France (75 percent) and Britain (25 percent)

1946 Britain and France agree to give their parts of Cameroon self-government or independence

1948 Nationalists in French Cameroon found the People's Union of Cameroon (UPC)

50–1959

1959 French Cameroon is granted internal self-government

60–1969

1960 Jan. 1 French Cameroon becomes the independent Republic of Cameroon. Alhaji Ahmadou Ahidjo of the UPC becomes president

1961 The southern part of British Cameroons and the Republic of Cameroon combine to form the Federal Republic of Cameroon. Northern British Cameroon votes to join Nigeria

1962 A UPC rebellion is put down by the Ahidjo regime

1966 Ahidjo forms the Cameroon National Union (CNU): all other parties are banned

70–1979

1972 Cameroon becomes a unitary (i.e. non-federal) state

1977 Cameroon becomes an oil exporting country

80–1989

1982 President Ahidjo resigns and is succeeded by Paul Biya

1984 An attempted coup by ex-president Ahidjo is defeated

1985 Biya renames the CNU the People's Democratic Movement

90–1999

1991 Political parties legalized

1992 Biya and the People's Democratic Movement retain power after Cameroon's first multiparty elections

1995 Cameroon joins the Commonwealth of Nations, a move seen partly as an attempt to placate the English-speaking minority

1998 Cameroon and Nigeria take a fishing rights dispute to the International Court

00–

2000 The World Bank approves a pipeline project to move oil from Chad to the coast of Cameroon

2001 Biya reorganizes the army following reports of growing discontent with the military

Njoya
He was the 17th king of the Bamum peoples, and was responsible for introducing the Islamic faith to Cameroon.

Christian missionary
Shortly after Cameroon became a German protectorate in 1884, the occupying forces attempted to impose their beliefs upon the indigenous peoples there.

Under foreign control
This stamp, issued in 1931, portrayed France as a civilizing influence.

© DIAGRAM

Central African Republic

In 1894, France created a territory called Oubangoui-Shari (present-da Central African Republic). In 1910, Oubangoui-Shari became part of a vast territory called French Equatorial Africa, which also included Cha French Congo and Gabon. Oubangoui-Shari became a French oversea: territory in 1946. In 1958, it gained internal self-government as the Central African Republic and it finally became an independent nation August 13, 1960. Before independence, the leading Central African politician was Barthélémy Boganda, who had served as prime minister But when Boganda was killed in a plane crash in 1959, he was succeed by the less experienced David Dacko. The country became a one-party state in 1962. However, it faced many problems and, in 1965, a coup brought General Jean Bédel Bokassa to power. In 1972, Bokassa made himself president for life and, in 1976, he renamed the country Central African Empire. In December 1977, he crowned himself Emperor Bokassa I. In September 1979, with French help, David Dacko led a coup which overthrew him. Dacko again made the country a republic.

Some people regarded Dacko as a puppet of France and, in 1981, he was replaced by General André Kolingba. His military regime banned political parties but, in 1992, Central African Republic adopted a multiparty constitution. In 1993, Kolingba was defeated in presidential elections by Ange-Félix Patassé, a former prime minister (1976–1978). In 1996, some soldiers staged a revolt because they had not received their wages. A second army uprising one month later led France to sen in troops to stop the rioting. Patassé set up a government of national unity and, in 1998, he agreed to replace the French troops with a UN-sponsored peacekeeping force. Patassé was reelected president in 1999

Anniversary
This stamp, issued in 1959, and showing President Boganda, commemorates the first anniversary of the creation of the Central African Republic.

Leaders

Bokassa, Jean Bédel
(1921–1996)
Bokassa, the army commander of Central African Republic, seized power in 1966. He served as president until 1976, when he made himself "Emperor" of the Central African Empire. A harsh dictator, in 1979 he was overthrown. He went into exile, but returned in 1986. He was tried and served six years in prison.

Dacko, David
(1930–)
David Dacko became the first president of Central African Republic in 1960. He was deposed in 1966 by Jean-Bédel Bokassa, but he returned to office in 1979 following a bloodless coup. Although committed to political liberalization, he attempted to curb opposition parties. In 1981, a military regime deposed Dacko.

Kolingba, André Dieudonné
(1936–)
André Kolingba, an army genera became head of state of Central African Republic in 1981, when h seized power from David Dacko a peaceful coup. After democrac was restored he was defeated b Ange-Félix Patassé in the 1993 elections. He was again defeated in the elections held in 1999, taking only 19% of the vote.

ntral African Republic (CAR) timeline

h century

	1805–1830 CE	The Baya people settle in the CAR region
	1889	The French establish an outpost at Bangui
	1894	The French create the territory of Oubangoui-Shari in present-day CAR
0–1949	**1910**	Oubangoui-Shari becomes part of French Equatorial Africa
	1949	Independence movement founded by Barthélémy Boganda
0–1959	**1958**	Oubangoui-Shari is granted internal self-government
0–1969	**1960 Aug 13**	Oubangoui-Shari becomes independent as Central African Republic David Dacko becomes the first president
	1962	Dacko makes the country a one-party state
	1966	Gen. Jean-Bédel Bokassa seizes power in a military coup
0–1979	**1972**	Bokassa becomes president for life
	1976	Bokassa appoints himself emperor and renames CAR the Central African Empire
	1979	Bokassa is overthrown by a French-supported coup
0–1989	**1987**	Bokassa is imprisoned for murder and embezzlement
0–1999	**1992**	A multiparty constitution is introduced
	1993	Ange-Félix Patassé becomes president after multiparty elections
	1996	France helps suppress a military rebellion
	1997	President Patassé calls for the withdrawal of French troops amid growing anti-French hostility
	1998	A UN force arrives in CAR to replace French troops
	1999	Patassé is reelected president, defeating Kolingba
0–	**2001**	An attempted coup is put down with Libyan help
	2002	President Patassé meets President Déby of Chad to discuss tensions between the two countries, including the use of bases in the Central African Republic by Chadian rebels

Jean Bédel Bokassa
He declared himself "Emperor" in 1976, and also renamed the Central African Republic the "Central African Empire."

Chad

Chad became a French protectorate (colony) in 1898. It became a French overseas territory in 1946 and an independent nation on August 11, 19[...]. The first president, Ngarta Tombalbaye, was a southerner. One problem facing him was the rivalry between the black southerners, many of whom are Christians, and the Muslim northerners. In 1962, the rebel National Liberation Front (FROLINAT) was formed in the north and war broke out in the 1960s. In the civil war, France aided the government while, from 1971, the rebels received aid from Libya, which claimed the Aozou strip on Chad's northern border. After Tombalbaye was killed in 1975, [...] was replaced by Félix Malloum. A new government, formed in 1978, contained an almost equal number of northerners and southerners. A former FROLINAT leader, Hissène Habré, became prime minister.

Fighting continued, mainly between groups in the north. Malloum fled the country in 1979. Two northern groups, one led by Habré and the other by the new president, Goukouni Oueddei, competed for power. Oueddei's forces, aided by Libya, took control. But in 1982, Habré became president. Oueddei returned to Chad in 1983 and, in 1986, Oueddei and Habré united to attack the Libyans. A truce was arranged [...] 1987, though no agreement was reached on the Aozou strip until the International Court of Justice ruled against Libya's claim in 1994. In 1990, a northern rebel group, the Patriotic Salvation Movement, overthrew Habré. The new president, Idriss Déby, introduced a multiparty system, He was elected in 1996 and reelected in 2001. His period in office began in 1998, when the Movement for Democracy and Justice in Chad rebelled in the north. A peace deal was signed in 2002, but fighting resumed when splits took place in the rebel movement.

Awaiting evacuation
These are victims of the civil war which took place in Chad in 1979.

Leaders

Déby, Idriss
(1952–)
Idriss Déby led the rebel forces that drove President Oueddei from office in 1982. He installed Hissène Habré as president, but, in 1990, he overthrew Habré and made himself president. After introducing a new democratic system, he was elected president in 1996, and was reelected to a second term in 2001.

Habré, Hissène
(1928–)
Habré was a leader of rebel forces in northern Chad in the 1970s. After serving as prime minister, his forces seized power in 1982. He served as president from 1982 until 1990, when he was deposed. Habré then fled to Senegal, where, in 2000, he was charged with torture and killings committed while he was Chad's head of state.

Tombalbaye, Ngarta
(1924–)
Ngarta Tombalbaye (formerly François Tombalbaye) became [...] first president of Chad when the country became independent in 1960. He served as president un[...] 1975 when he was assassinated during an army coup and was succeeded by Félix Malloum. He had earlier served as prime minister.

ad timeline

e-19th century

c. 5000 CE	Rock paintings show scenes of hunting in the Sahara desert
8th century	Berber peoples from the north migrate to Chad
11th century	Kanem Kingdom begins to develop northeast of Lake Chad
c. 1100	Islam is introduced to the region by Arab merchants
13th century	Kanem merges with the neighboring kingdom of Bornu

h century

1808	The Hausa invade Kanem–Bornu
1890	Kanem-Bornu, Baguirmi and Wadai are conquered by the Sudanese leader Rabeh
1898	France declares Chad a protectorate

)0–1949

1908	Chad becomes part of French Equatorial Africa
1930	Cotton farming begins in Chad
1935	France agrees to cede the Aozou strip to the Italian colony of Libya but the agreement is never implemented

50–1959

1958	Chad achieves internal self-government

50–1969

1960	**Aug 11** Chad becomes independent of France: François Tombalbaye is the first president
1962	Chad becomes a one-party state
1965	Civil war breaks out after northern rebels form the *Front de Libération National du Tchad* (FROLINAT)

70–1979

1971	Libya begins to support FROLINAT rebels
1973	Libya occupies the Aozou strip in northern Chad
1975	President Tombalbaye is killed during a military coup: Gen. Félix Malloum becomes president
1979	Efforts to establish a government of national unity end in failure

80–1989

1982	Hissène Habré becomes president
1984	Famine due to prolonged drought
1986	FROLINAT–Libyan alliance breaks down
1987	The government establishes its authority in the north, except for the Libyan-occupied Aozou strip

90–1999

1990	President Habré overthrown by a Libyan-supported coup: Gen. Idriss Déby becomes president and promises to introduce democracy
1993	New legislature appointed to oversee transition to democracy
1994	Libya agrees to withdraw from the Aozou strip after a ruling by the International Court
1996	Déby is elected president
1998	A new rebellion led by the Movement for Democracy and Justice (MDJC) breaks out in the north

)00–

2000	Habré is placed under house arrest in Senegal and charged with torture
2001	Déby is reelected president, winning 63 percent of the vote, amid accusations of electoral irregularities
2002	A peace deal is signed with the MDJC, but fighting breaks out when talks are halted by divisions in the rebel movement

Rock paintings
These depict scenes of hunting and herding in the region of the present-day Sahara Desert c. 5000 BCE.

Spoils of war
Rabib bin Fadl Allah resisted French colonial invaders from 1899, but was eventually killed at the Battle of Lakta on April 22, 1900.

©DIAGRAM

Congo, Democratic Republic of

In 1908, the Belgian government took over the mineral-rich Congo Free State (now the Democratic Republic of Congo) and renamed it the Belgian Congo. The country became independent as the Republic of the Congo on June 30, 1960. Almost immediately, the country was plunged into conflict by army revolts, ethnic conflicts, and the secession of two mineral-rich provinces, Kasai and Katanga. The country was reunited in 1963. In 1964, Moïse Tshombe, the Katangan leader, became prime minister and, in 1965, his coalition won a victory in national elections. But the army seized power in 1965 and General Joseph Désiré Mobutu became president. He made the country a one-party state in 1970 and, in 1971, he renamed it Zaïre. Mobutu was a corrupt dictator, but his anti-Communist views made him useful to western powers.

In 1990, Mobutu allowed political parties to be formed, though elections were repeatedly postponed. In 1996, after the ethnic conflicts in Burundi and Rwanda had spilled over into eastern Zaïre, Laurent Kabila led Tutsi rebels living in Zaire in a rebellion against Mobutu. Kabila was supported by Uganda and Rwanda, because both feared an attack by Hutu forces based in Zaïre. Mobutu fled the country in May 1997. Kabila became president, renaming the country the Democratic Republic of Congo. But Kabila fell out with his former allies. Rwanda and Uganda, together with Burundi, supported rebel groups to overthrow him. Civil war began in 1998. Forces from Angola, Chad, Namibia, and Zimbabwe arrived to support Kabila, creating a major conflict. In July 1999, a peace accord failed to halt the fighting. Kabila was assassinated in January 2001. He was succeeded by his son, Major-General Joseph Kabila. Hopes of a peace deal rose, but the civil war continued.

Making a point
Two demonstators protest against the prime minister, Patrice Lumumba, in 1960. He was jailed later that same year, and murdered in Katanga the following year.

Leaders

Kabila, Laurent Désiré
(1939–2001)
In 1996, Kabila became head of the Alliance of Democratic Forces for the Liberation of Congo-Zaïre, consisting mainly of Tutsis. Kabila became president of the country, which he renamed the Democratic Republic of Congo, in May 1997. He was assassinated by a bodyguard in 2001 and was succeeded by his 31-year-old son, Joseph.

Mobutu Sese Seko
(1930–1977)
Originally named Joseph Désiré Mobutu, Mobutu Sese Seko adopted his Africanized name in 1971. He served as president from 1965–1997, when he fled the country accused of corruption. He ruled in a dictatorial manner, holding the country together despite the many ethnic groups which threatened to pull it apart.

Tshombe, Moïse Kapenda
(1919–1969)
Moïse Tshombe led the "Republic of Katanga" (now the province of Katanga) that declared itself independent from the rest of the country in 1960. After UN troops occupied the province in 1963, Tshombe went into exile. He returned in 1964 and became the country's head of state. But he was deposed in 1965 and went into exile.

ngo, Democratic Republic of, timeline

-19th century

1483 CE	Portuguese navigator Diogo Cão discovers the mouth of the Congo River
16th century	Kongolo people found the Luba kingdom in southern Congo
18th century	Kuba kingdoms develop in central Congo region

h century

1874–1877	Henry Morton Stanley follows the course of the Congo River
1878	King Leopold of Belgium employs Stanley to investigate the potential of the Congo region for colonization
1884	The Berlin Conference on Africa recognizes King Leopold as sovereign of the Congo Free State

0–1959

1908	The Belgian government takes over administration of the Congo Free State
1957	Belgians permit the formation of African political parties

0–1969

1960 Jun 30	Congo becomes an independent republic under Joseph Kasavubu
1960 July	Katanga province secedes
1960 Sept	Kasavubu dismisses and jails his prime minister Patrice Lumumba
1961	Lumumba is murdered in Katanga
1963	Katanga is forcibly reunited with the rest of the country
1965	Gen. Joseph-Désiré Mobutu becomes president after a coup

0–1979

1970	Mobutu declares the country a one-party state
1971	Congo is renamed Zaire, the capital Leopoldville is renamed Kinshasa
1977	Rebellion in Shaba province (formerly Katanga) is put down with French assistance
1978	A second rebellion in Shaba province is put down

0–1989

1984	Mobutu is re-elected president in elections in which he is the only candidate
1986	CIA uses Zaire as a base for supplying arms to UNITA rebels in Angola

0–1999

1990	Mobutu lifts the ban on political parties
1991	Economic problems lead to widespread rioting
1994	One million Hutu refugees flee to Zaïre from Rwanda
1995	Outbreak of the deadly Ebola virus in Kikwit
1996	Hutu-Tutsi conflict in Rwanda and Burundi spreads to the Tutsi of eastern Zaïre
1997	Laurent Kabila overthrows the Mobutu government and becomes president with the support of Tutsi forces: name of the country is changed to Democratic Republic of Congo
1998	Civil war breaks out. Angola, Chad, Namibia and Zimbabwe send forces to support Kabila against rebels supported by Burundi, Rwanda and Uganda

0–

2001	Kabila is assassinated in January and is succeeded by his son, Major-General Joseph Kabila
2002	Congo and Rwanda sign a peace accord

King Leopold II
He established the Congo Free State in 1885 and, in 1908, the country was renamed the Belgian Congo.

President Kasavubu
1960 saw Kasavubu become the first president of the Democratic Republic of Congo.

Joseph Kabila
He became president upon the assassination of his father in 2001.

© DIAGRAM

Congo, Republic of

In 1880, an area north of the Congo River became a French protectora called French Congo. It was renamed Middle Congo in 1903 and, in 1910, it became part of French Equatorial Africa. This huge territory a included Chad, Gabon, and Oubangoui-Shari (later Central African Republic). In 1946, Middle Congo became an overseas territory of France and, on August 15, 1960, it became fully independent as the Republic of Congo. The first president, Abbé Fulbert Youlou, was for to resign in 1963, following his attempts to curb the opposition. His successor, Alphonse Massamba-Débat set up a one-party system in 19 The army arrested Massamba-Débat in 1968 and Major Marien Ngoua became head of state. In 1970, Ngouabi declared Congo to be a Marxi Leninist (Communist) country, though it kept good relations with Fran

Ngouabi was assassinated in 1977. A military council took control a appointed Colonel Joachim Yhombi-Opango president. In 1979, the military council was abolished. Yhombi-Opango resigned and Colone Denis Sassou-Nguesso became president. In 1990, Congo abandoned Communist policies and, in 1991, opposition parties were legalized. Sassou-Nguesso remained president, but with greatly reduced powers. With the country moving towards a market economy, democracy was restored in 1992 and free elections were held. Pascal Lissouba became president. However, in 1997, fighting broke out when the government tried to disarm Sassou-Nguesso's private militia. Sassou-Nguesso's forces seized Brazzaville and Pointe-Noire. Lissouba fled into exile ar Sassou-Nguesso became president. Conflict again erupted in January 1999 when militias loyal to Lissouba attacked Brazzaville. A peace agreement was signed in November 1999.

Pascal Lissouba
He became president in 1992 in the first free elections since democracy was restored in the country.

Leaders

Ngouabi, Marien
(1938–1977)
Marien Ngouabi deposed Alphonse Massamba-Débat in a coup in 1968. He became president in 1970. He tried to develop Congo into a Marxist-Leninist (Communist) state, but ethnic rivalries and power struggles made Congo unstable, and Ngouabi was assassinated in 1977.

Sassou-Nguesso, Denis
(1943–)
Denis Sassou-Nguesso became president of Congo in 1979. In 1990, he renounced Marxist-Leninism and, in 1991, legalized opposition parties. He was defeated in elections in 1992. He returned to power in 1997, and was again reelected president in a landslide victory in the elections in 2002.

Youlou, Abbé Fulbert
(1917–1972)
A Roman Catholic priest, Fulbe Youlou became the first preside of Congo in 1959. He adopted dictatorial measures to maintain his authority. In 1963, he was forced to resign following the arrest of trade union leaders. This action, caused widespread unrest and a general strike.

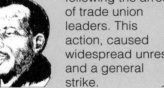

...ngo, Republic of, timeline

...-19th century

1483 CE Portuguese navigator Diogo Cão discovers the mouth of the Congo River

...h century

1874–1877 Henry Morton Stanley explores the course of the Congo River

1875 French explorer Pierre Savorgnan de Brazza explores the region

1880 De Brazza and the Bateke king Makoko sign a treaty making the region north of the Congo River a French protectorate

1891 Colony of French Congo created

...0–1949

1903 French Congo becomes known as Middle Congo

1910 Middle Congo becomes part of the colony of French Equatorial Africa

1921–1935 Up to 20,000 African forced laborers die during construction of the Congo-Ocean railway

1940 Middle Congo supports the Free French in World War II

1946 French end the practice of forced labor

...0–1959

1958 Middle Congo is granted internal self-government

...0–1969

1960 Aug 15 Congo becomes an independent republic: Fulbert Youlou becomes the first president

1963 Labor uprising overturns the Youlou government

1964 Congo becomes a one-party state

1969 A group of army officers under Capt. Marien Ngouabi seizes power

...0–1979

1970 Congo declares itself a Marxist country and is renamed People's Republic of Congo

1977 Ngouabi is assassinated: Col. Jaochim Yhombi-Opango succeeds

1979 Yhombi-Opango resigns: Col. Denis Sassou-Nguesso becomes president

...0–1989

1988 Conference in Brazzaville paves the way for Namibia's independence

...0–1999

1990 Congo renounces Marxism

1991 Political parties are legalized

1992 A new multiparty constitution is approved by a referendum: the country resumes its old name, Republic of Congo

1993 President Sassou-Nguesso is defeated in elections by Pascal Lissouba

1997 Sassou-Nguesso seizes power with the support of Angolan troops

1998 The Republic of Congo and the Democratic Republic of Congo begin negotiations for the demarcation of their common frontier

1999 Further fighting is concluded by a concord between the government and rebel forces.

...0–

2002 Sassou-Nguesso wins a landslide victory in the first presidential elections in Congo since 1992.

French Congo
In 1880 the French explorer, Pierre de Savorgnan de Brazza, signed a treaty with the Bateke king, Makoko, which made the region north of the Congo River into a French protectorate. De Brazza is shown here being entertained at the court of the king.

Anniversary
This stamp, issued by the Republic of Congo in 1975, celebrated the 25th anniversary of the Chinese People's Republic, an ally of Congo in its attempt to create a Marxist-Leninist state.

© DIAGRAM

Djibouti

Ready for battle
An Afar (or Danakil) man is shown here in traditional dress.

In 1888, France acquired an area which now contains the city of Djibouti, a port built to rival British Aden in Yemen. The French unite this area with other nearby areas and turned them into a territory called French Somaliland. In 1892, Djibouti became capital of this territory. 1967, a vote was held on the territory's status. The Issa favored independence, but the Afar wanted to keep ties with France. A majorit of the people voted to remain French and the territory was renamed th French Territory of the Afars and Issas. Another vote in the 1970s resulted in a large majority for independence and the Republic of Djibouti was born on June 27, 1977.

Djibouti's first president, Hassan Gouled Aptidon, faced many problems arising from the tensions between the Afar and the Issa peoples. In 1981, Djibouti adopted a one party system, the sole party being the People's Rally for Progress (RPP). In 1991, Afar rebels belonging to the Front for the Restoration of Unity and Democracy (FRUD) began a guerrilla war against government forces. FRUD declared a ceasefire in 1992 and, later that year, Djibouti adopted a constitution allowing for multiparty politics. Fighting resumed in late 1992 and early 1993 but, in May 1993, Gouled was reelected presiden In 1994, FRUD signed a "Peace and National Reconciliation Agreement," which allowed for the formation of a national coalition government, the revision of the electoral roll, and the integration of FRUD militants into the army and civil service. In elections in 1997, a coalition formed by the RPP and FRUD won all the seats in the Cham of Deputies (parliament). In 1999, Gouled's nephew, Ismail Omar Guelleh, the nominee of the RPP, was elected president.

Leaders

Gouled Aptidon, Hassan
(1916–)
Hassan Gouled Aptidon became the first president of Djibouti when it achieved its independence in 1977. He was reelected in 1981, 1987 and 1993. He did not seek reelection in 1999 and he was succeeded by his nephew Ismail Omar Guelleh. Gouled Aptidon was born into an Issa (Somali-related) nomadic family and he became an Issa leader. He servedin both the French Senate and Assembly. As president, he

sought to reduce ethnic rivalry between the Issa and Afar people, who are ethnically related to people in Ethiopia. He appointed several Afars to serve as vice-presidents. But he reacted sharply to the guerrilla activities of the opposition FRUD party against his government.

Guelleh, Ismail Omar
(1947–)
Guelleh was elected president Djibouti in April 1999, following decision of his uncle President Hassan Gouled Aptidon not to seek the nomination for a fourth term. Guelleh had served as the country's head of security. He favored close links with France and wanted to reconcile the interests of various factions in Somalia.

outi timeline

	3rd century CE	Ancestors of the Afar people migrate to the Djibouti area from Arabia
	825	The Afars are converted to Islam
	14th century	Kingdom of Adal dominates the Djibouti region
	1415	Christian Ethiopians kill the Muslim ruler of Saylac (near modern-day Djibouti city)
	1527	Ahmed Gran of Adal invades Ethiopia
	1543	Ahmed Gran killed in battle with an Ethiopian-Portuguese army
	18th century	Somali Issa people migrate into the southern Djibouti region
h century		
	1862	France purchases the Afar port of Obock
	1881	France establishes a coaling station for ships at Obock
	1884	France signs protectorate agreements with the sultans of Obock and Tadjoura
	1888	France establishes the colony of French Somaliland
	1896	Newly developed port of Djibouti city becomes the capital of French Somaliland
	1897	Djibouti becomes the official port of trade for Ethiopia
0–1949	**1917**	A railway is completed from Djibouti to the Ethiopian capital, Addis Ababa
	1924–1934	Road building program opens up the interior of Djibouti
	1946	Djibouti is granted a representative council and a deputy in the French national assembly
	1947	Issa nationalists begin a campaign for independence
0–1959	**1958**	French Somaliland is granted internal self-government
0–1969	**1967**	French Somaliland votes to remain a French territory and is renamed the French Territory of the Afars and Issas
0–1979	**1977**	**Jun 27** Afars and Issas become the independent republic of Djibouti after a referendum: Hassan Gouled Aptidon becomes the first president
	1979	The Afar Popular Liberation Movement is banned
0–1989	**1981**	Djibouti becomes a one party state
	1988	Ethiopia and Somalia recognize Djibouti's borders
	1989	Fighting breaks out between Afars and Issas in Djibouti city and Tadjourah
0–1999	**1991**	Guerrilla warfare breaks out between the Afars and Issa dominated government forces
	1992	President Gouled Aptidon introduces a multiparty constitution
	1993	Gouled Aptidon re-elected in multiparty elections
	1994	Afars and Issas reach a peace agreement
	1996	Exiled opponents of the Gouled Aptidon regime are abducted from Addis Ababa
0–	**2001**	Work is completed on Djibouti's port, increasing its capacity by 50 percent

Colonial legacy
A French gunboat is shown on this postage stamp.

A call to arms
This poster, issued in 1940–1941, attempted to persuade black Africans to join the French colonial forces.

Egypt

A wedding celebration
This stamp, issued in 1951, marked the union of King Farouk I and Queen Narriman.

The Suez Crisis, 1956
This cartoon depicted the nations in conflict.

A victorious Israel
Egypt and Syria were defeated by Israel in the Yom Kippur War, 1973.

Egypt became independent in 1922, but Britain kept many powers, including the right to keep troops in the country. In 1948, Egyptian an other Arab armies fought against the newly-created State of Israel. Isr proved victorious and many Egyptians, including army officers, blam their government. In 1952, a military rebellion in Egypt overthrew Ki Farouk I and Egypt became a republic in 1953.

In 1954, General Muhammad Neguib was replaced as prime ministe by Colonel Gamal Abd an-Nasser. In the same year, Britain agreed to withdraw its troops from the Suez Canal zone. In 1956, Nasser, now president, seized the Suez Canal after Britain and the US refused to he Egypt build the Aswan High Dam. Britain, France and Israel then invaded the Sinai peninsula and the Canal region. But, under pressure from the United States, the Soviet Union and other powers, the invasi forces withdrew from the Canal zone. Nasser suffered a setback when Egypt lost further territory to Israel in 1967. However, he continued to serve as president until his death in 1970.

In 1973, Egyptian and Syrian forces launched an attack on the Sinai peninsula, but its troops were pushed back to the Suez Canal. Nasser': successor, Muhammad Anwar al Sadat, sought peace with Israel, whic was achieved in 1979. Under the agreement, Egypt regained the Sinai peninsula. Extremists assassinated Sadat in 1981. His successor, Muhammad Hosni Mubarak, continues to play a major role in Middle Eastern affairs. At home, Islamic fundamentalists disliked what they s as the westernization of Egypt and their attacks on foreign visitors damaged the tourist industry in the 1990s. Tourism was again hit in 20 following the terrorist attacks on New York and Washington.

Leaders

Mubarak, Muhammad Hosni (1928–)
Mubarak became president of Egypt following the assassination of Muhammad Anwar al Sadat in 1981. Mubarak had earlier served as vice-president from 1975. He dealt firmly with Islamic extremists and survived several assassination attempts. He also sent troops to defend Saudi Arabia after Iraq's invasion of Kuwait in 1999.

Nasser, Gamal Abd an- (1918–1970)
Nasser served as prime minister of Egypt from 1954 to 1956, and as president from 1956 until 1970. He pursued policies aimed at raising living standards. When he nationalized the Suez Canal in 1956, he provoked much anger in the West, but his response was admired by most Arab countries.

Sadat, Muhammad Anwar al (1918–1981)
Sadat became president of Egy on the death of Gamal Abd an-Nasser in 1970. He launched a peace initiative that led to the C David treaty in 1979. His work fc peace earned him and the then Israeli prime minister Menachim Begin the Nobel Peace Prize in 1978. He was assassinated by Muslim extremists in 1981.

pt timeline

639–642 CE	Muslim Arabs conquer Egypt
1171	Saladin becomes ruler of Egypt
1250–1517	The Mamluk dynasty rules Egypt
1517	The Ottoman Turks conquer Egypt
1798	Napoleon invades Egypt

n century

1801	French troops in Egypt surrender to a British and Ottoman army
1805	Muhammad Ali (Ali Pasha) seizes power in Egypt
1859–1869	Construction of the Suez Canal
1875	Egypt sells its share in the Suez Canal to Britain
1882	Britain annexes Egypt

0–1949

1914	Britain makes Egypt a protectorate
1922	Britain grants Egypt nominal independence
1923	Egypt becomes a constitutional monarchy
1942	British defeat the Italians and Germans at the battle of El Alamein
1945	Egypt is a founder member of the Arab League
1948	Egypt and other Arab countries invade Israel
1949	Egypt accepts an armistice with Israel

0–1959

1952	King Farouk is deposed by a military coup
1953	Egypt becomes a republic
1954	Gamal Abd an-Nasser becomes president of Egypt
1954	Britain agrees to withdraw its troops from the Suez Canal zone
1956	Suez Crisis: Israel, Britain and France invade after Nasser announces the nationalization of the Suez Canal
1958	Egypt and Syria form the United Arab Republic (UAR)

0–1969

1960	Construction begins on the Aswan High Dam
1961	Syria withdraws from the UAR
1967	Egypt, Syria and Jordan defeated by Israel in the Six-Day War
1968	Aswan High Dam completed

0–1979

1970	Death of Nasser: Anwar al-Sadat succeeds him as president
1973	Egypt and Syria are defeated by Israel in the Yom Kippur War
1977	Sadat visits Jerusalem in search of a peace accord
1978	Camp David accords between Egypt and Israel
1979	Egypt and Israel sign a peace treaty

0–1989

1981	President Sadat is assassinated: Hosni Mubarak succeeds him as president

0–1999

1990–1991	Egypt joins the US-led coalition against Iraq in the Gulf War
1997	Islamic fundamentalist terrorists kill 60 western tourists
1999	Hosni Mubarak is re-elected as president

0–

2001	The United States places several Egyptians on its "most wanted" list of terrorists. An estimated 13,000 Islamic extremists are held in prison in Egypt

Napoleon in Egypt
During 1798–1799 French troops, under the leadership of Napoleon, tried to block Britain's trade route to India via Egypt.

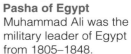

Pasha of Egypt
Muhammad Ali was the military leader of Egypt from 1805–1848.

Death of Sadat, 1981
The president of Egypt was assassinated by Islamic fundamentalists.

© DIAGRAM

Equatorial Guinea

Anniversary
This stamp celebrates the second anniversary of the independence of Equatorial Guinea.

In 1959, Spanish Guinea, as the country was then known, was reorganized to form two Spanish provinces. In 1963, the two province renamed Equatorial Guinea, were granted a degree of self-governmen Equatorial Guinea became an independent republic on October 12, 19 The first president, Francisco Macías Nguema, made the country a on party state in 1970 and, in 1971, he became president for life. His rule was tyrannical and many of his opponents were assassinated. Around third of the population, including many of the most skilled, emigrated This caused economic chaos. In 1979, Macías Nguema was overthrov and executed. His successor was his nephew, Lt.-Col. Teodoro Obiang Nguema Mbsango, who ruled through a Supreme Military Council. H released 5,000 political prisoners and restored links with Spain and th United States. In 1982, he revived some democratic institutions, but th Supreme Military Council remained the sole political body. In 1983, elections were held for a new parliament.

Despite the reforms, Obiang Nguema kept supreme control and the government was accused of human rights abuses. A single political pa – the Democratic Party of Equatorial Guinea (PDGE) – was formed in 1987 and, in 1992, a multiparty system was introduced. The ruling PDGE won 1993 elections, after most opposition parties had called fo boycott. Obiang Nguema was reelected in 1996 in what observers cal a "farcical" poll, because most opposition candidates had withdrawn. Parliamentary elections in 1999 resulted in another victory for the PDGE, again amid protests that the election was unfair. The economy improved after 1992, when oil was first produced. However, observer alleged that little of the revenue from oil reached the national treasury

Leaders

Macías Nguema, Francisco
(1922–1979)
Francisco Macías Nguema served as the first president of Equatorial Guinea between 1968–1979. He was a brutal dictator who launched a reign of terror, ordering many political murders. His term in office ended in a military coup led by his nephew, Teodoro Obiang Nguema. Following the coup, Nguema was tried and executed.

Mbsango, Teodoro Obiang Nguema
(1942–)
In 1979, Brigadier-General Teodoro Obiang Nguema Mbsango overthrew his uncle Francisco Macías Nguema in a military coup and became president of Equatorial Guinea. He had earlier served as governor of the island of Fernando Po (now Bioko). He was promoted to command the national guard in 1975 and became involved in his uncle's program state terrorism. As president, he released more than 5,000 politi prisoners and obtained aid from Spain and France. But power remained highly centralized, despite the introduction of a multiparty system. He was reelected in 1996, with more th 99 percent of the vote. His opponents had withdrawn, alle irregularities during the electora process.

atorial Guinea timeline

-19th century
c. 1200 CE	Bubi people from the mainland settle Bioko island
1472	Fernão do Po sights Bioko and claims it for Portugal
1777–1778	Portugal cedes its claim to the area to Spain by the treaties of San Ildefonso and Pardo

n century
1843–1858	Spain conquers the area and establishes the colony of Spanish Guinea

0–1949
1900	The borders of Spanish Guinea are fixed by the Treaty of Paris
1936	The colony supports Franco in the Spanish Civil war

0–1969
1968	**Oct. 12** The country becomes independent as Equatorial Guinea: Macías Nguema becomes the first president

0–1979
1970	A one-party dictatorship is declared
1979	Lt.-Col. Teodoro Obiang Nguema Mbsango seizes power in a military coup: Macías Nguema is executed

0–1989
1985	Guinea joins the franc zone, tying its currency to the French monetary system
1987	The Democratic Party of Equatorial Guinea is formed

0–1999
1992	A multiparty constitution is introduced
1993	The Democratic Party wins 68 of 80 seats in elections
1996	Obiang Nguema is reelected as president amid allegations of vote rigging
1998	Mass arrests of Bubi separatists on the island of Bioko
1999	National elections are won by the ruling Democratic Party amid accusations of fraud

0–
2001	The economy grows quickly because of oil exploitation
2002	Equatorial Guinea and Nigeria sign an agreement over the utilization of offshore oil on their maritime boundaries

Tribute to a leader
This stamp, issued in 1961, celebrates the 25th anniversary of General Franco as head of state. He was supported by Spanish Guinea in the civil war in Spain in the 1930s.

© DIAGRAM

Eritrea

Eritrea became an Italian colony in 1890. In 1941, the British drove t͏ Italians out of Eritrea. Britain then ruled Eritrea until 1952, when the voted to make the area a self-governing part of Ethiopia. Ethiopia trie prevent opposition by banning political parties and trade unions. But Eritrean nationalists set up the Eritrean Liberation Front (ELF) which began a guerrilla struggle for independence in 1961. In 1962, many Eritreans were angered when Ethiopia turned their territory into a province. From 1970, the Eritrean People's Liberation Front (EPLF) gradually replaced the ELF as the main guerrilla force. In 1974, a military government, led by Lt.-Col. Haile-Mariam Mengistu, took ov in Ethiopia. The EPLF continued its struggle and it took over large ar͏ in Eritrea, setting up social services and schools. Ethiopia's governme was gradually weakened by war and droughts. Finally in 1991, Eritre͏ Tigrean and other forces overthrew Mengistu's regime. Rebels from Tigre province set up a new government in Addis Ababa, while the Eritreans formed their own government in their capital, Asmara.

Eritrea became independent on May 24, 1993, with Issias Afewerki its first president. In 1994, the EPLF turned itself into a political party called the People's Front for Democracy and Justice and, in 1997, Afewerki was reelected. In December 1995, Eritrea had a brief confli͏ with Yemen over the Hanish islands in the Red Sea, but, in 1998, the World Court ruled that the islands belonged to Yemen. Eritrea's relati͏ with Ethiopia remained friendly until 1998, when fighting broke arou͏ the town of Badme on Eritrea's southwestern border. This conflict continued into 2000. In 2002, an international body ruled on the dispu͏ borders. Both countries claimed that their rulings were in their favor.

An independent nation
A stamp, issued in 1995, marking Eritrea's newly-acquired status.

Leaders

Afewerki, Issias
(1945–)
Issias Afewerki abandoned his studies in 1966 in order to become a guerrilla in the struggle against the Ethiopian government of Haile-Mariam Mengistu, which had refused to negotiate on Eritrean demands for independence. He first joined the Eritrean Liberation Front (ELF). But, in 1970, he joined the Eritrean People's Liberation Front (EPLF) and was given the job of commanding one of the movement's fighting units. From 1987, Afewerki served as secretary-general, and the effective leader, of the EPLF. In 1991, he became chairman of a provisional government. His government prepared the country for the 1993 referendum (vote) which was held on the issue of independence. Afewerki became Eritrea's first president when the country became independent in May 1993. He was reelected in 1997. A former follower of Marxist ideas, President Afewerki abandoned Communist policies. In office, he faced many problem͏ restructuring his war-damaged country. However, in the early 2000s, he was criticized for his suppression of newspapers an͏ individuals who opposed him.

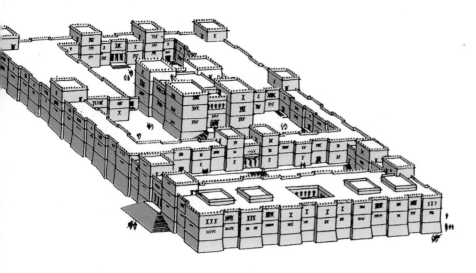

Ts'akha Maryam
This is a reconstruction of the palace complex which was located at Axum in the Tigre region of Ethiopia.

rea timeline

c.1–975 CE		The kingdom of Axum dominates the region of present-day Eritrea
n century		
1882–1889		Italy conquers Eritrea
0–1949	**1935**	Italians use Eritrea as a base for their conquest of Ethiopia
	1941	The British expel the Italians from Eritrea
0–1959	**1952**	Under a UN agreement, Eritrea is federated with Ethiopia
0–1969	**1961**	Civil war breaks out between the Eritrean Liberation Front (ELF) and the Ethiopian government
0–1979	**1970**	Eritrean People's Liberation Front (EPLF) replaces the ELF as the main Eritrean resistance movement
0–1989		
	1987–1988	EPLF victories end Ethiopian control in Eritrea
0–1999	**1991**	Eritrean and Tigrean rebels overthrow the Ethiopian government
	1993	**May 24** Eritrea becomes independent: Issias Afewerki of the EPLF becomes president
	1995	Eritrea clashes with Yemen over the ownership of the Hanish islands in the Red Sea, but, in 1998, the World Court rules that the islands belong to Yemen
	1998–1999	Armed clashes along the Ethiopian border
0–	**2000**	Eritrea and Ethiopia sign a peace treaty to end the border conflict
	2002	An international body rules on Eritrea's disputed borders. Both Eritrea and Ethiopia claim success in their territorial demands

Resistance
This is the insignia of the EPLF (Eritrean Popular Liberation Front) which fought against Ethiopian control of Eritrea.

©DIAGRAM

Ethiopia

Military coup
Major Haile-Mariam Mengistu (far left) seized power in 1974.

Guerrilla fighters
These ethnic Somalis, from the southern region of Ogaden opposed the Ethiopian government in 1977.

Ethiopia, one of Africa's oldest nations, was never colonized. Its mod history began when Haile Selassie I became emperor in 1930. Italy invaded the country in 1935 and Haile Selassie went into exile. Howe he returned in 1941 at the head of a British-Ethiopian force, which defeated the Italians. Haile Selassie tried to reform his country, but the reforms came slowly. In 1952, Eritrea (formerly Italian Somaliland) w federated with Ethiopia. In 1962, Ethiopia made Eritrea a province, bu many Eritreans objected. They started a 30-year war for independence After a famine caused by droughts, military leaders overthrew the emperor in 1974. They declared Ethiopia to be a socialist republic wit Lt.-Col. Haile-Mariam Mengistu as head of state. His regime faced problems arising from Ethiopia's many ethnic groups. Besides the wa Eritrea, the government had to contend with the opposition of many Tigre people. They also had to combat the ethnic Somalis, supported t Somalia, in the Ogaden region. The war continued in Ogaden until 19

Eritrean and Tigrean forces overthrew Mengistu's regime in 1991. T Tigrean-dominated Ethiopian People's Revolutionary Democratic Fro (EPRDF) set up a government in the capital. It was headed by Meles Zenawi, who became prime minister. Eritrea became independent of Ethiopia in 1993 and, in 1994, Ethiopia adopted a new constitution. It divided the country into nine regions, giving the largest ethnic groups some control over their own affairs. At first, Ethiopia's relations with Eritrea were friendly. However, in 1998, Eritreans and Ethiopians fou along a disputed border in the northwest. A ceasefire was agreed in 20 An international panel ruled on the disputed areas in 2002. Both partie claimed that they gained the areas they had wanted.

Leaders

Haile Selassie I
(1892–1975)
Originally named *Ras Tafari*, Haile Selassie I served as emperor of Ethiopia from 1930 until 1974. He went into exile in 1935 when Italy occupied Ethiopia, but he returned in 1941. He was a reformer but his caution provoked criticism. He was revered as divine by the Rastafarian religious group which was named after him.

Mengistu, Haile-Mariam
(1937–)
Lt.-Colonel Haile-Mariam Mengistu seized power from Haile Selassie I in 1974. He made Ethiopia a republic and became its first president. He followed socialist policies and received aid from the former Soviet Union. But his regime was marked by famine and civil war. He was overthrown in 1991 and took refuge in Zimbabwe.

Zenawi, Meles
(1955–)
Meles Zenawi was a guerrilla leader in the struggle against Ethiopia's military leader Haile-Mariam Mengistu. In 1991 he w elected head of the governmen the Council of Representatives. This council was set up by the Ethiopian People's Revolutionary Democratic Front. He was reelected in 1994.

iopia timeline

c. 1–975 CE	The kingdom of Axum dominates northern Ethiopia
c. 350	King Ezana of Axum becomes the first African ruler to be converted to Christianity
639–642	Arab conquest of Egypt cuts Ethiopia off from the rest of the Christian world
1492	The Portuguese make contact with the Emperor of Ethiopia
1557	A Jesuit mission is sent to Ethiopia
16th century	Ethiopia fragments into small semi-independent kingdoms
1632	Jesuits expelled for undermining the Orthodox church

h century

1855	Emperor Tewodros II reunifies Ethiopia
1868	Tewodros commits suicide after a British punitive expedition captures his fortress at Magdala
1889	Emperor John killed fighting the Mahdists of the Sudan: he is succeeded by Menelik II
1896	Menelik defeats an Italian invasion at Adowa

0–1949

1916	Emperor Lij Yasu is overthrown after he converts to Islam
1923	Ethiopia becomes a member of the League of Nations
1930	Ras Tafari becomes emperor; adopts name Haile Selassie
1931	Haile Selassie gives Ethiopia a written constitution
1935	Italy invades Ethiopia
1941	The British drive the Italians out of Ethiopia

0–1959

1952	Eritrea is federated with Ethiopia by the UN

0–1969

1961	Eritrean rebels begin a war of independence
1962	Ethiopia formally annexes Eritrea

0–1979

1972–1974	Prolonged drought leads to devastating famine
1974	Emperor Haile Selassie overthrown by a military coup: Lt.-Col. Haile-Mariam Mengistu becomes president and adopts Marxist policies
1974	An insurrection breaks out in Tigre province
1975	Haile Selassie dies in prison
1977	Somalia invades the disputed Ogaden region of Ethiopia

0–1989

1984-1987	Prolonged drought causes famine on a massive scale
1988	Ethiopia and Somalia sign a peace treaty

0–1999

1991	Mengistu regime overthrown by Eritrean and Tigrean rebels
1992	The Tigrean-dominated Ethiopian People's Revolutionary Democratic Front (EPRDF) forms a transitional government
1993	Ethiopia recognizes Eritrea's independence
1994	A new constitution gives the provinces the right to secede
1995	The EPRDF wins the first elections under the new constitution
1998–2000	Armed clashes along the Eritrean border

0–

2000	Ethiopia and Eritrea sign a peace treaty
2002	An international panel rules on the border disputes. Both Ethiopia and Eritrea claim victory

Menelik II
A king of Shoa (a province of Ethiopia), he became Emperor of Ethiopia in 1889.

The Battle of Adowa
Ethiopian forces defeated the Italian army at this battle in 1896, thus preserving the independence of their country.

© DIAGRAM

Gabon

In 1910, Gabon became a territory in French Equatorial Africa, a vast region that also included what are now Central African Republic, Cha and the Republic of Congo. In 1946, Gabon became a separate French overseas territory. Full independence was achieved on August 17, 196 The first president was Léon M'Ba, leader of the *Bloc Démocratique Gabonais* (BDG). M'Ba had been a leading nationalist, although his critics regarded him as pro-French and conservative. In 1964, M'Ba w overthrown in a coup led by his main rival, Jean-Hilaire Aubame, But French troops intervened and restored him to power. M'Ba's increasin authoritarian rule ended when he died in office in 1967.

M'Ba's successor Albert-Bernard Bongo adopted Islam in 1973 and changed his name to Omar Bongo. In 1968, Bongo made the country one-party state, with the Gabonese Democratic Party (PDG) as the so party. At first, Bongo's rule was authoritarian and conservative. Yet Gabon's political stability and its economy, which was based on priva enterprise, helped to attract foreign investment. Gabon developed its r mineral resources, including oil and natural gas, manganese and uranium. An economic crisis occurred in the mid-1970s. Bongo stabilized finances, but political opposition mounted. In 1989, Bongo decided to open up the political system. In 1990, the government legalized opposition parties and, later that year, the PDG won a majori of the seats in the National Assembly. In 1993, Bongo was reelected president, but the opposition parties did not accept the result. A coaliti government was formed in 1994 but, in 1996, the PDG won a large parliamentary majority. In 1998, Bongo was returned as president and 2001, the PDG won another large majority in national elections.

Anniversary
This stamp, issued in 1965, and depicting President M'Ba, marks the fifth anniversary of independence.

Omar Bongo
This bank note, issued in 1985, shows Omar Bongo who was reelected a number of times to the role of president of Gabon.

Leaders

Bongo, El Hadj Omar
(1935–)
Omar Bongo was formerly known as Albert-Bernard Bongo. He was appointed vice-president in 1965 and he became president in 1967 on the death of President M'Ba. He also served as prime minister from 1968 until 1976. He believed strongly in free trade and private enterprise and his economic policies attracted foreign investors to the country. He made Gabon a one-party state in 1968. Despite some discontent, especially when economic downturn occurred, he managed to maintain the country's stability. However, in the late 1980s, increasing civic unrest led him to introduce much more democratic systems. Multiparty politics was restored in 1990. Bongo was reelected president in 1993 and again in 1998. His party, the PDG, has controlled the National Assembly since 1990.

M'Ba, Léon
(1902–1967)
Léon M'Ba was the leading figu in the struggle for independenc He became president in 1960, having served as head of the government from 1957–1960. H survived an attempted coup in 1964, aided by the French, and was reelected in 1967. He died later that year, succeeded by Omar Bongo.

...on timeline

...-19th century

...3th century CE	The Mpongwe people settle in Gabon
c 1800	The Fang begin to settle in Gabon
1472	Portuguese explore the coast of Gabon

...h century

1839	France establishes a naval and trading post on the present site of Libreville
1849	A group of freed slaves is settled at the station which is named Libreville (free town)
1875	The Fang emerge as the dominant ethnic group in Gabon
1883	Libreville becomes the capital of the French colony of Gabon
1885	The Berlin conference recognizes French control of Gabon
1889	Gabon becomes part of the French colony of Middle Congo (now Republic of Congo)

...0–1949

1910	Gabon becomes a territory of French Equatorial Africa
1940	Gabon supports the Free French in World War II
1946	Gabon is given an elected legislature

...50–1959

1957	Gabon is given internal self-government

...60–1969

1960 Aug 17	Gabon becomes independent: Léon M'Ba is the first president
1964	An attempt to overthrow M'Ba is crushed by French troops
1967	M'Ba dies in office: succeeded by Bernard-Albert Bongo
1968	Bongo declares Gabon a one-party state

...70–1979

1973	Bongo is reelected president and changes his name to El Hadj Omar Bongo
1974	Construction of the Trans-Gabon railroad begins
1975	Gabon becomes a member of OPEC
1977	Gabon supports an unsuccessful military coup in Benin
1979	Bongo is reelected president in elections in which he is the only candidate

...80–1989

1982	The opposition National Reorientation Movement is suppressed
1984	Bongo gives France permission to build a nuclear plant in Gabon
1986	Bongo is again reelected president in elections in which he is the only candidate
1989	Riots follow the murder of Joseph Redjambe, the leader of the Gabonese Progressive Party, in Libreville

...90–1999

1990	Opposition parties are legalized: the ruling Gabonese Democratic party wins the assembly elections
1993	Bongo retains the presidency after winning first multiparty elections
1996	Gabon withdraws from OPEC
1998	Bongo wins presidential elections with 66 percent of the vote

...00–

2001	The Gabonese Democratic Party wins an overwhelming victory in legislative elections
2001–2002	An outbreak of the deadly Ebola virus causes alarm

Fang warrior
As the 19th century drew to an end, the Fang had become the dominant ethnic group in Gabon.

Albert Schweitzer
He studied medicine so that he could work as a missionary doctor. Together with his wife, a nurse, they set up a hospital at Lambaréné on the Ogowe River in French Equatorial Africa, of which Gabon became a part in 1910.

©DIAGRAM

The Gambia

The coastal area of what is now The Gambia became a British colony i 1843. Britain made the interior a protectorate (colony) in 1893. By 190 Britain ruled the entire area of the present-day Gambia. After World W II, Britain tried to develop the economy. But political development was slow and confined mainly to the Bathhurst (now Banjul) area. The Protectorate People's Society was reformed by Sir Dawda Jawara as th People's Progressive Party in 1959, It was the first to draw support from people in the interior. The Gambia became independent on February 18 1965. In 1970, the country became a republic, with Jawara as president

The government worked to develop the economy, including tourism, and establish close relations with Senegal, which almost surrounds The Gambia. In 1967, The Gambia and Senegal concluded a treaty of association. In 1981, after an attempted coup in The Gambia, Senegale troops helped to put down the rebels. The Gambia and Senegal then set the Confederation of Senegambia in 1982. Under this confederation, bo countries integrated their military and monetary resources but remained independent. However, the confederation was dissolved in 1989.

In 1994, Captain Yahya Jammeh deposed Jawara. Jammeh became head of a military government and all political activity was ended. Civilian rule was restored in 1996. A new party, the Alliance for Patrio Reorientation and Construction (APRC), was set up. Presidential elections in 1996 resulted in a victory for Jammeh, while the APRC wo a majority in the National Assembly in 1997. Political parties active when Jawara was president were barred from taking part in the electior In the late 1990s, Jammeh was criticized for his government's abuses o human rights, but he was reelected in 2001.

An independent nation
This stamp, issued in 1975, celebrated the tenth anniversary of the independence of The Gambia.

Leaders

Jammeh, Captain Yahya
(1965–)
Jammeh joined the army in 1984 and became an officer in 1989. He achieved the rank of captain in 1994 and seized power during a bloodless military coup in The Gambia in 1991. At first, he ruled the country as head of the Armed Forces Provisional Ruling Council. He was elected president in 1997, and he was reelected in 2001.

Jawara, Alhaji Sir Dawda Kairaba
(1924–)
Sir Dawda Jawara served as prime minister of The Gambia from 1963 until 1970, when the country became a republic. From 1970 until 1994, he served as the country's president. He survived several coups, but he was finally deposed by a military group in 1994. At college, Jawara studied veterinary science. He entered politics in 1959 when he transformed the Protectorate People's Society into the People's Progressive Party. (PPP) which governed The Gambia from independence until 1994. Jawar; was committed to democratic rule and resisted calls to make the country a one-party state. He favored close ties with Senegal, though Gambian fears of Senegalese domination prevented political unification.

Gambia timeline

-19th century

h–15th century	The Gambia region is part of the Mali empire
1455 CE	Portuguese set up trading posts on the coast
1618	Portugal sells its rights in the area to England
1642	France sets up a trading post on the Gambia River
1644	The English start buying slaves from the Gambia region
1661	The English found a trading post on James Island in the Gambia river
1658	James Island ceded to the Dutch
1665–1667	England recaptures James Island in the Second Dutch War
1763	Britain expels the French from the Gambia and Senegal region
1765	Britain creates the colony of Senegambia, incorporating parts of Gambia and Senegal
1783	Britain cedes Senegal to France

h century

1807	The Gambia loses economic importance when Britain abolishes the slave trade
1816	British merchants found Bathurst (now the capital Banjul)
1843	Britain sets up the colony of Gambia
1866–1888	Gambia governed as part of the colony of Sierra Leone
1870–1876	Britain negotiates with France to exchange Gambia in return for concessions elsewhere
1889	Present borders of Gambia agreed by treaty with France
1893	Britain proclaims the interior a protectorate

00–1949

1902	All of modern Gambia is under British control
1906	Slavery in Gambia is abolished
1945	The Gambia gains limited internal self-government

60–1969

1963	The Gambia gains full internal self-government
1965	**Feb 18** The Gambia becomes independent

70–1979

1970	Gambia becomes a republic: Dawda Jawara becomes the first president
1970	Development of tourist industry begins

80–1989

1981	A military coup is defeated with the aid of Senegal
1982	The Gambia and Senegal form the Confederation of Senegambia with joint armed forces
1985	Jawara refuses to sign a treaty promoting closer ties with Senegal
1989	The Confederation of Senegambia is dissolved after disputes between The Gambia and Senegal

90–1999

1991	The Gambia and Senegal sign a reconciliation treaty
1994	Jawara overthrown by a military coup: Yahya Jammeh becomes president
1996	Jammeh wins presidential elections under a new constitution
1997	Multiparty elections for a National Assembly

00–

2000	Relations with Senegal deteriorate after the peaceful change of government in that country
2001	Jammeh is reelected president

Propaganda
This 18th-century engraving reflected the depth of feeling about the issue of slavery.

A former colony
This stamp was issued in 1869 when The Gambia was still governed as part of the colony of Sierra Leone.

©DIAGRAM

Ghana

By 1872, Britain controlled the coast of what is now Ghana (then calle
the Gold Coast). In 1874, Britain made the area a British colony, while
in 1901, Britain took over land to the north. After World War I, Britain
was mandated to rule the western part of the former German Togoland
This area, called British Togoland, became part of the Gold Coast in
1956. Kwame Nkrumah became prime minister of Gold Coast in 1952
He led his country to independence on March 6, 1957, when Gold Co:
was renamed Ghana, the first black African colony to win its freedom.
Nkrumah, who was admired by many black Africans, became preside
when Ghana became a republic in 1960. However, in 1964, Ghana
became a single-party nation, looking increasingly for Communist
support. Nkrumah became more authoritarian as the economy weaken

Nkrumah was overthrown in 1966. The ruling military council
dismissed the parliament. The new head of government, General Josep
Ankrah, served until 1969, when Ghana held free elections. Kofi Busi
leader of the Progress Party, became prime minister. After another cou
in 1972, Colonel Ignatius Acheampong became head of state. But he v
forced to resign in 1978, when General Frederick Akuffo replaced him
In 1979, yet another coup brought Lieutenant Jerry Rawlings to power
civilian government was elected in 1979 but, in 1981, Rawlings staged
another coup. In 1991, Rawlings announced a return to a multiparty
system. Under a new constitution, Rawlings, candidate of the National
Democratic Congress (NDC), was elected president. He was reelected
president in 1996, but he retired in 2000. In elections in 2000, John
Agyekum Kufuor defeated the NDC candidate and became president.
His New Patriotic Party also won a majority in parliament.

Broken statue
Nkrumah was
overthrown in a military
coup in 1966, a fall from
grace mirrored by this
broken statue in Accra.

Leaders

Nkrumah, Dr Kwame
(1909–1972)
Nkrumah became prime minister in
1951 and president of Ghana,
when the country became a
republic in 1960. He was deposed
by a military coup in 1966. He
supported the creation of a
socialist United States
of Africa. He was
widely admired until
his autocratic rule
made him unpopular
in Ghana.

Kufuor, John Agyekum
(1938–)
Kufuor, leader of the New Patriotic
Party, was elected president of
Ghana in December 2000,
defeating the candidate of the
ruling NDC. Kufuor had earlier held
positions as deputy prime minister
and secretary for local
government. His
government's first task
was to tackle
Ghana's severe
economic
problems.

Rawlings, Jerry John (J.J.)
(1947–)
Son of a Scottish father and a
Ghanaian mother, Rawlings seiz
power in Ghana in 1979, but he
ruled for only 112 days before
restoring civilian government. B
he again seized power in
1981. In 1992, he was
elected president
under a multiparty
system and he was
reelected in 1996.
He retired from
politics in 2000.

ana timeline

-19th century
1471 CE	Portuguese navigators explore the region which they name the Gold Coast
1637–1642	The Dutch capture Portuguese bases on the Gold Coast
1651	Danes establish trading posts on the Gold Coast
1664	English merchants establish headquarters at Cape Coast Castle

h century
1824–1826	First British-Asante War: Britain occupies the Asante capital, Kumasi
1874	The Second British-Asante War: British forces sack Kumasi and the Gold Coast is declared a British colony
1893–1894	Defeated in the Third British-Asante War, the Asante accept a British protectorate
1895–1896	Fourth British-Asante War: the British put down an Asante uprising

0–1949
1900	The last Asante resistance to the British is extinguished
1901	British protectorate established over northern Ghana
1922	The western part of German Togoland is mandated to Britain by the League of Nations: it is administered as part of Ghana

0–1959
1951	Ghana gains full internal self-government
1952	Kwame Nkrumah becomes prime minister of Gold Coast
1956	In a UN-sponsored referendum, British Togoland votes for full union with Gold Coast
1957 **Mar. 6**	Gold Coast becomes independent as Ghana

0–1969
1960	Ghana becomes a republic: Nkrumah becomes first president
1965	Akosombo dam begins production of hydroelectric power
1966	Nkrumah is ousted by a military coup: Gen. Joseph Ankrah becomes head of government
1969	Ankrah resigns and is replaced by Brigadier Akwasi Amankwa Afrifa who restores civilian rule

70–1979
1972	Col. I. K. Acheampong becomes head of government after a military coup
1978	Acheampong resigns and is replaced by Gen. Frederick Kwasi Akuffo
1979	Akuffo is overthrown in coup led by Lieut. Jerry Rawlings. Afrifa, Acheampong and Akuffo are executed and a civilian government is elected

80–1989
1981	Rawlings seizes control of the government in another coup: political parties are outlawed

90–1999
1992	Rawlings is elected president under a new multiparty constitution
1996	Rawlings reelected president

00–
2000	Opposition leader John Agyekum Kufuor is elected president following the retirement of Rawlings
2002	Ministers resign amid accusations that they had backed one of two clans involved in fighting in the north

Rebellions
There were four Asante-British wars between 1824–1896, and rebellions continued until 1901.

Consular visit
In 1819 the British Consul visited Kumasi to resolve a dispute between the Asante king and the British Company of Merchants.

Independence
A strip of cloth woven to mark the independence of Ghana in 1957. The inlay picture shows the inkpot and pen used to sign the document.

©DIAGRAM

Guinea

In 1881, the ruler of Futa Jalon in what is now northern Guinea placed his state under French protection. This territory was called Rivières du Sud until 1890, when it was separated from Senegal. It was later called French Guinea and became part of French West Africa. In 1946, Guinea became a French overseas territory. But in 1958, the people voted again joining the French Community and Guinea became an independent republic on October 2, 1958. The first president was a socialist, Ahmad Sékou Touré, leader of the Democratic Party of Guinea (PDG). After independence, with the country in chaos after France's rapid withdraw the PDG became the only political party. At first, Guinea turned to Communist countries for trade and aid. But from 1961, the United States became the main supplier of aid and investment. Relations with France were restored in 1963, but Touré's rule became oppressive. The situation improved in the late 1970s, when many political prisoners were released.

After Touré's death in 1984, military leaders took over the government Their leader was Lansana Conté, who became head of state, leading a military council. Conté introduced free market policies and strengthened economic ties with France. He abolished the most repressive of Touré's laws, but, gradually, he became more dictatorial. By the early 1990s, the economy had begun to improve. In 1991, political parties were legalized and Conté was elected president in 1993. In 1994, Conté's Party for Unity and Progress won a majority in the National Assembly. Conté was reelected president in 1998. In the late 1990s, Guinea was troubled by wars in neighboring Liberia and Sierra Leone. In 2001, Guinea faced a major crisis as refugees from the wars sought sanctuary in Guinea.

Independence or not?
General De Gaulle held a referendum on a new constitution for France and her overseas territories in 1958. Official government posters urged the citizens to vote yes to France; over these were pasted a request to vote no, which was effectively a demand for independence.

Leaders

Conté, Lansana
(1945–)
Conté seized power in Guinea in 1984 in a bloodless coup a few days after the death of President Sékou Touré. At first, he introduced liberal policies. But after a failed coup in 1985, his rule became oppressive. He introduced a multiparty system in 1991 and was elected president in 1993 and 1998.

Touré, Ahmad Sékou
(1922–1984)
Sékou Touré became president of Guinea in 1958, when his country became independent. He had been a major figure in the struggle for independence in black Africa. Like his fellow nationalist, Kwame Nkrumah in Ghana, he supported socialist policies. He was also a Pan-Africanist, who believed that African nations should come together to form a United States of Africa. After independence, when France withdrew all its assistance and aid, Touré made his country one-party state. From 1971, following an unsuccessful invasion by opposition forces in neighbor Guinea-Bissau, Touré adopted increasingly repressive policies. However, he improved his human rights record before his death in 1984.

nea timeline

19th century		
11th century CE	Guinea region forms part of the Ghana empire	
16th century	Guinea region forms part of the Mali empire	
18th century	Kingdom of Futa Jalon develops in western Guinea	
h century		
	1849	France establishes control of the coast of Guinea
	1865	Eastern Guinea forms part of Samouri Touré's Mandinke empire
	1881	Futa Jalon becomes a French protectorate
	1886–1892	France conquers the Mandinke empire
	1895	The area of Guinea is incorporated into French West Africa
	1898	Samouri Touré is captured by French forces and exiled
0–1949	**1947**	Democratic Party of Guinea (PDG) founded to campaign for independence
0–1959	**1952**	Sékou Touré becomes leader of the PDG
	1958 Oct 2	Guinea rejects French offer of internal self-government and votes for independence: Touré becomes president.
0–1989	**1984**	On the death of Touré, the army under Col. Lansana Conté seizes power
0–1999	**1990**	Conté appoints a transitional government to oversee a return to civilian rule
	1993	Conté narrowly retains the presidency in multiparty elections
	1998	Conté is reelected president
0–	**2001**	Guinea becomes involved in a refugee crisis caused by civil wars in Liberia and Sierra Leone. Voters support a proposal to extend the presidential term from five to seven years

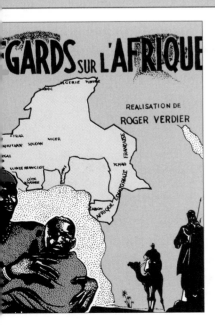

An empire in Africa
This film poster from the 1930s identifies the substantial part of northwest Africa which was then under the control of the French colonial powers.

Guinea-Bissau

In the nineteenth century, Portugal ruled what are now Guinea-Bissau and the Cape Verde islands under one governor. But, in 1879, Portugal separated the two areas. The mainland area, named Portuguese Guinea and Cape Verde both became Portuguese overseas provinces in 1951. 1956, the formation of the African Party for the Independence of Guinea and Cape Verde (PAIGC) marked the start of a guerrilla war against Portuguese rule. Portuguese Guinea became independent as Guinea-Bissau on September 10, 1974. Luiz Cabral, the first president, was unable to solve the country's economic problems. In 1981, the prime minister, João Vieira, overthrew Cabral and became leader of the ruling military Revolutionary Council. Cape Verde broke off relations with Guinea-Bissau and the Cape Verde branch of the PAIGC, which had wanted to unify the two nations, was dissolved. Several unsuccessful coups occurred in the 1980s. A National Assembly was elected in 198 and it made Vieira president, though Guinea-Bissau was a single-party state until 1991. From 1986, the government liberalized the economy.

In national elections in 1994, Vieira was elected president, defeating Kumba Ialá, leader of the Party for Social Renewal (PRS). But the economy remained weak. In 1998, Vieira dismissed Ansumane Mane, army chief of staff, for allegedly helping rebels in Casamance, a provin in Senegal bordering Guinea-Bissau. Mane's dismissal led to an army mutiny and a civil war lasting 11 months. In May 1999, a military coup led by Mane overthrew Vieira. In elections in 1999 and 2000, the PRS won a majority in parliament and Kumba Ialá was elected president. Mane was killed in 2000 while he was allegedly trying to stage a coup. In 2001, the government announced that it had put down another coup.

Amilcar Cabral
Assassinated in 1973, he was a leader in the struggle for Guinea-Bissau's independence from Portuguese rule.

Leaders

Cabral, Amílcar Lopes
(1931–1973)
Amilcar Cabral was leader of the independence struggle against Portuguese rule in Portuguese Guinea. He was one of the six founders of the African Party for the Independence of Guinea and Cape Verde (PAIGC) in 1956.However, he was assassinated in 1973 and his brother Luiz became the country's first president.

Cabral, Luiz de Almeida
(1929–)
Luiz Cabral was one of the six founders of the PAIGC. He was prominent in the independence struggle and he became the country's first president when Guinea-Bissau achieved independence in 1974. He promoted the interests of Cape Verdeans while the economy declined, and was deposed in 1980.

Vieira, João Bernardo
(1939–)
João Vieira overthrew Luiz Cabral in 1980 and became the head of state. He became executive president in 1984 and was reelected in 1989. In 1994, he was elected president in multiparty elections, but he was deposed in 1999. He was succeeded by Malam Bacai Sanha who became interim president.

nea-Bissau timeline

-19th century

1480 CE	Portugal founds trading posts on the Guinea coast
1687	Portuguese found Bissau city as a fortified center for the slave trade

h century

1879	The region becomes the Portuguese colony of Portuguese Guinea

50–1959

1951	Portuguese Guinea becomes an overseas province of Portugal
1956	Nationalists form the *Partido Africano da Independência do Guiné e Cabo Verde* (PAIGC)

50–1969

1963	PAIGC begins a war of independence

70–1979

1974	**Sept 10** Portuguese Guinea becomes independent as Guinea-Bissau: Luiz Cabral is the first president

80–1989

1980	Cabral overthrown by a military coup: Maj. João Bernardo Vieira becomes president
1984	A new constitution creates a National People's Assembly and Council of State

90–1999

1991	The law making the PAIGC the sole political party is abolished
1994	PAIGC wins Guinea-Bissau's first multiparty elections: Vieira retains the presidency
1997	Guinea-Bissau adopts the CFA *franc* as its official unit of currency – replacing the *peso*
1998–1999	An army revolt causes widespread disturbance in Bissau

00–

2000	Kumba Ialá is elected president
2001	In December, the government announces that it has thwarted an attempted coup by army officers

A proud heritage
In the 19th century the interior of western Africa was dominated by Fulani states. This present-day Fulani cavalryman, and horse, are adorned in full ceremonial dress.

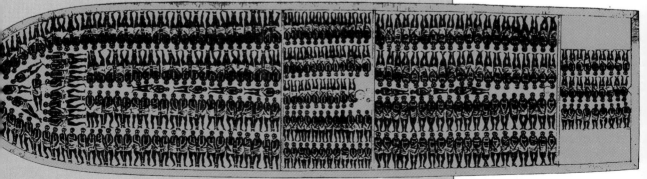

Floor plan of a slaver
Many slave ships, packed like this one, sailed from Guinea-Bissau, which was an important center of slave transportation to the New World.

Ivory Coast

The area that is now Ivory Coast (officially Côte d'Ivoire) became a French colony in 1893. In 1904, it became part of French West Africa, which also included what are now Benin, Burkina Faso, Guinea, Mali, Mauritania, Niger, and Senegal. In 1946, the French made Ivory Coast self-governing territory in the French Union and, on August 7, 1960, the country won its independence. The first president was Félix Houphouët-Boigny, whose rule was paternalistic and pro-Western. But, for most of his time in office, the country prospered, enjoying steady economic growth. The president's rule was based on a one-party system – the one party was the Ivory Coast Democratic Party (PDCI)). Not all of the PDCI's policies were popular. In 1983, the president's birthplace, Yamoussoukro, was designated as the country's new capital, though many government offices remained in Abidjan. One of the world's largest Christian churches, costing an estimated US $800 million, was built in Yamoussoukro in the 1980s. At the time, Ivory Coast was facing severe economic problems, arising partly from the falling prices for the country's exports, notably cocoa and coffee.

Opposition parties were legalized in 1990 and Houphouët-Boigny was reelected president and his party took most of the seats in the National Assembly. Houphouët-Boigny died in December 1993 and Henri Konan Bédié became head of state. Bédié was elected president in 1995, but, in December 1999, an army mutiny occurred. To restore order, General Guei, the country's former military chief, removed Bédié from office. In elections in 2000, the two main candidates were Guei and Laurent Gbagbo. When it became clear that he was losing, Guei cancelled the poll. But Gbagbo declared himself president and Guei fled the country.

Massacre
On October 29, 2000, the bodies of at least 55 young men were found in a forest near Abidjan. They were Muslims and also supporters of Alassane Outtara, the opposition leader who had been defeated in recent elections.

Leaders

Bédié, Henri Konan
(1934–)
Henri Konan Bédié, the former speaker of the National Assembly of Ivory Coast, became the country's head of state following the death of President Félix Houphouët-Boigny in December 1993. He was reelected president in 1996, but he was overthrown in a coup and Brigadier-General Robert Guei became president.

Gbagbo, Laurent
(1945–)
Laurent Gbagbo declared himself president in October 2000, when the former head of state, Brigadier-General Guei, tried to cancel the results of the presidential poll. In the 1970s, Gbagbo spent two years in prison , then eight years in exile in the 1980s, but he returned in 1988 to campaign for multiparty democracy.

Houphouët-Boigny, Félix
(1905–1933)
Born in Yamoussoukro, the official capital, Félix Houphouët-Boigny was the first president of Ivory Coast in 1960. He served until his death in 1993. As president, he ruled in a paternal manner, and made his country one of the most stable in Africa, but it became less stable in the late 1990s.

ry Coast timeline

e-19th century

1637 CE French missionaries visit the Ivory Coast

:th century

1830s French trading posts established along the Ivory Coast
1887–1889 France reaches protectorate agreements with local rulers
1893 France claims Ivory Coast as a colony
1898 Present borders of Ivory Coast fixed after the capture of Samouri Touré

)0–1949 **1908** Military occupation of Ivory Coast completed
1914–1918 Frequent rebellions as France tries to conscript Africans to fight in World War I
1932 Most of the colony of Upper Volta (now Burkina Faso) is added to Ivory Coast
1944 Félix Houphouët-Boigny and Auguste Denise form the African Farmers Union (SAA),
1946 The African Democratic Union (RDA) is founded to campaign for independence for France's African colonies
1946 Ivory Coast and Upper Volta are separated

i0–1959 **1950** Under the leadership of Houphouët-Boigny, the RDA begins a policy of cooperation with France
1958 Ivory Coast gains internal self-government

i0–1969 **1960 Aug. 7** Ivory Coast becomes independent: Houphouët-Boigny becomes the first president
1963 An attempted military coup is defeated

'0–1979 **1973** Another attempted military coup is defeated

30–1989 **1980** An attempted military coup is defeated
1981–1985 An agricultural recession causes growth of the national debt
1983 Work starts on a new capital at Yamoussoukro (Houphouët-Boigny's birthplace)
1987 Economy badly hit by 50 percent fall in the price of cocoa
1989 The largest Christian church in Africa is completed at Yamoussoukro

)0–1999 **1990 Mar.** After tax rises cause rioting, a new multiparty constitution is introduced
1990 Oct. Houphouët-Boigny wins the first presidential elections held under the new constitution
1993 Houphouët-Boigny dies and is succeeded by Henri Konan Bédié
1995 Bédié wins presidential elections held under rules that barred his main opponents
1999 Bédié is overthrown and a military regime is established under General Robert Guei

)0– **2000 Mar.** Laurent Gbago is elected president, defeating Guei
2001 Accusations are made that Ivorian cocoa farmers are buying migrant child laborers and are using them virtually as slaves

Taking a break
King of the Bonboukou, Adjommani, is shown here with his two sons.

Largest church in the world
This is the Basilica of Our Lady of Peace. It was constructed between 1987–1989, and was commissioned by President Félix Houphouët-Boigny.

© DIAGRAM

Kenya

A democratic right
Muslim Kenyan women queue up to vote in fresh elections.

Bomb at US embassy
An explosion in Nairobi in 1998 killed over 230 people and wounded thousands more.

Known first as British East Africa, Kenya became a British colony in 1920. In 1952, the Mau Mau rebellion broke out among the Kikuyu people, Kenya's largest single ethnic group. Kenya's most prominent African leader, Jomo Kenyatta, was convicted in 1953 of leading the Mau Mau movement, a charge he denied. He was freed from prison in August 1961 and a coalition government was set up. Kenya became independent on December 12, 1963 with Jomo Kenyatta as the first prime minister. He became president in 1964 when Kenya became a republic. The new government introduced policies to help black Africans, though non-Africans who became Kenyan citizens had equal status. In 1967, the East African High Commission, set up by the Briti in 1948, was transformed into the East African Community. But relatic between Kenya and its partners, Tanzania and Uganda, deteriorated an the Community was dissolved in 1977. It was not until November 199 that the Community was revived.

After Kenyatta's death in 1978, the vice-president, Daniel arap Moi, took over as president. In 1982, the government made Kenya African National Union (KANU) the only legal political party. The governmer was accused of corruption and using repressive methods. But Moi was reelected in 1983 and 1988 and 1992, when multiparty elections were held. The 1992 elections were marred by accusations of fraud, but, in 1997, the first balanced elections since independence were held. Moi again reelected president. In November 2002 a bomb, attributed to al Qaida, killed 11 people at an hotel in Mombasa. In December 2002 Mwai Kibaki was elected president, ending 39 years of domination by the Kenyan African National Union.

Leaders

Kenyatta, Jomo
(1889–1978)
Jomo Kenyatta served as prime minister of Kenya (1963–1964) and as president (1964–1978). He was arrested in 1952 and imprisoned for his alleged involvement in managing the Mau Mau rebellion against white rule. He was released in 1959 but then spent another two years under house arrest.

Kenyatta, Margaret Wambui
(1928–)
The daughter of the Kenyan leader Jomo Kenyatta, Margaret Kenyatta became an active campaigner on behalf of women in the developing world, During her father's imprisonment, she helped him keep in touch with his supporters. She entered politics in 1960 and became mayor of Nairobi (1970–1976).

Moi, Daniel arap
(1924–)
Daniel arap Moi served as vice-president of Kenya from 1967 ur 1978, when he succeeded Jom Kenyatta as president. His party the Kenya African National Unio was the sole legal party from 1982 until 1991. Although his government was criticized for corruption he was reelected in 1992 and 1997.

Kenya timeline

	c. 1000 CE	Arab merchants introduce Islam to the East African coast
	1498	Portuguese navigator Vasco da Gama reaches Kenya via the Cape of Good Hope
h century		
	1861	Control of the Kenyan coast passes to Zanzibar
	1888	The Imperial British East Africa Company is formed
	1890	An Anglo-German treaty fixes the southern border of the Imperial British East Africa Company's territory
	1895	The British government dissolves the Imperial British East Africa Company and establishes the East Africa Protectorate
0–1949	**1901**	The British build a railroad from Mombasa to Lake Victoria, opening up the Kenyan highlands for white settlers
	1920	The interior of Kenya becomes a British Crown Colony; the coast is a protectorate, nominally ruled by the Sultan of Zanzibar
	1947	Jomo Kenyatta becomes leader of the Kenya African Union (KAU), which had been founded in 1944
50–1959	**1952**	The Mau Mau terrorists begin attacks on white settlers and African supporters of British rule
	1953	Kenyatta is convicted of being a Mau Mau leader and jailed
	1956	Mau Mau movement is suppressed by the British
	1957	The first Africans are elected to the colonial legislature
60–1969	**1961**	Kenya African National Union (KANU) wins elections to a new parliament but it refuses to take office unless its leader Kenyatta is released from jail. Kenya African Democratic Union (KADU) takes office instead
	1963 Dec. 12	Kenya becomes independent with Kenyatta as prime minister
	1964	Kenya becomes a republic with Kenyatta as president. KADU merges with KANU to make Kenya a one-party state
	1967	Kenya, Tanzania and Uganda form the East African Community
	1969	Kenyatta dissolves the Kenya People's Union (KPU)
70–1979	**1977**	The East Africa Community is dissolved
80–1989	**1982**	A new constitution makes KANU the only legal party
90–1999	**1991**	Under pressure from aid donors, a multiparty constitution is introduced
	1992	Moi and KANU win presidential and parliamentary elections held under the new constitution amid allegations of fraud
	1997	Moi is reelected president with 40 percent of the vote
	1998	A car bomb explosion outside the US embassy in Nairobi kills 250 people
	1998	Kenya, Tanzania and Uganda set up a new East African Community, aimed at creating a common market
00–	**2001**	A bill to combat corruption is defeated in parliament
	2002	Terrorist bomb in Mombasa kills 11 people. Mwai Kibaki is elected as president

Taking a rest
Indian workers were imported to help build the East Africa Railway.

Making a point
Mau Mau supporters often went to great lengths for effect.

Mau Mau rebellion
Imprisonment in detention camps awaited those captured by the authorities.

©DIAGRAM

Lesotho

In 1820, southern Africa was disrupted by wars caused by the rise of t[...] Zulu kingdom. Some refugees fled to what is now Lesotho, where a c[...] named Moshoeshoe offered them protection. By 1824, he had united them into the Basotho nation. From 1856, the Basotho fought off attac[...] by South African Boers (Afrikaners). In 1868, Moshoeshoe asked Bri[...] for protection. The territory, known as Basutoland, then became a Brit[...] protectorate (colony). In 1964, Basutoland became a constitutional monarchy. In 1965, Chief Leabua Jonathan was elected prime ministe[...] and Paramount Chief Moshoeshoe II, direct descendant of the founde[...] the nation, Moshoeshoe I, became king. Basutoland became independ[...] as the Kingdom of Lesotho on October 4, 1966.

Moshoeshoe II wanted extra powers but Jonathan made him accept [...] ceremonial role. In 1970, Jonathan placed the king under house arrest. Moshoeshoe left the country but soon returned. Relations with South Africa became strained when Jonathan opposed its racial policies. In 1986, the army overthrew Jonathan and a military group, led by Majo[...] General Justin Lekhanya, took control. They turned over executive power to Moshoeshoe II. But when the king tried to undermine the general's position, Lekhanya made Moshoeshoe's son, Letsie III, king[...] 1991, Lekhanya was forced out of office. In 1992, the veteran politici[...] Ntsu Mokhehle was elected prime minister. Moshoeshoe returned hon[...] and, in 1995, he was restored to the throne. But after he was killed in [...] accident in January 1996, Letsie III returned as monarch. Charges of electoral fraud led to an army mutiny. The prime minister requested South African troops to restore order. The troops withdrew in 1999. Bethuel Mosisili was reelected in May 2002.

Ceremonial attire
King Letsie III, who ruled Botswana from 1990–1995, and then again in 1996, is shown here in his regal robes.

Leaders

Jonathan, Chief (Joseph) Leabua
(1914–1987)
A great-grandson of Moshoeshoe I, Chief Leabua Jonathan was Lesotho's leading nationalist leader before independence. He then became Lesotho's first prime minister when his country became independent in 1966. He ruled the country as prime minister until 1986 when he was overthrown by a military coup.

Letsie III
(1964–)
Crown Prince David Mohato Bereng Seeiso was made king, with the title Letsie III, by the military government which ruled the country in 1990. He agreed to abdicate in 1995 to allow his father, King Moshoeshoe II, to return as king. When his father was killed in an automobile crash, he again became king.

Moshoeshoe II
(1938–1996)
Moshoeshoe II became king of Lesotho in 1960. In 1970, he we[...] into exile for eight months after clashing with the prime minister Chief Leabua Jonathan. He was deposed in 1990 and exiled by the military government. He was restored to the throne in January 1995, but was killed in an automobile accident in 1996.

...otho timeline

c. 1818 CE	Chief Moshoeshoe of the Moketeli leads a coalition of peoples into present-day Lesotho to escape the Zulu conqueror Shaka
c. 1824	Moshoeshoe unites his followers into the Basotho nation
1856–1868	Boers attempt to conquer the Basotho
1868	Basotho appeal to Britain for protection against the Boers
1869	Britain establishes the protectorate of Basutoland
1870	Death of Moshoeshoe
1871	Basutoland comes under the administration of the British Cape Colony (now in South Africa)
1880	The Basotho rebel against British efforts to disarm them
1884	Britain reestablishes control of Basutoland
1910	The Basutoland Council of chiefs and elected representatives is formed
1943	Nine district councils are established as advisory bodies
1944	Britain declares that the Council and the paramount chief will be consulted before any legislation is enacted
1956	Basutoland is granted full internal self-government
1960	Basutoland is given its first constitution
1964	The constitution is revised to provide for a constitutional monarchy
1965	In general elections under the new constitution, Chief Leabua Jonathan of the Basutoland National Party (BNP) becomes prime minister. Paramount chief Motlotlehi Moshoeshoe II becomes king
1966 Oct. 4	Basutoland becomes the independent kingdom of Lesotho
1970	Chief Jonathan suspends the constitution after early election returns show the BNP is about to lose power
1983	South African saboteurs attempt to destroy the country's main power plant
1986	Chief Jonathan is overthrown by a South African-backed military coup. Maj. Gen. Justin Lekhanya becomes head of government
1990	The military government forces king Moshoeshoe II to abdicate in favor of his son Letsie III
1991	Lekhanya is forced to resign and is replaced by Col. Elias P. Ramaema
1993	Multiparty constitution introduced. Basotho Congress Party (BCP) under Ntsu Mohehle wins power
1995	King Letsie III abdicates in favor of his father Moshoeshoe II
1996	King Moshoeshoe II is killed in an automobile accident: Letsie III returns to the throne
1998	Rioting follows a disputed election result and South African troops restore order
2000	Letsie III marries in a Roman-Catholic wedding, breaking his family's tradition of polygamy

(Left margin period labels: 00–1949, 50–1959, 60–1969, 70–1979, 80–1989, 90–1999, 00–)

Moshoeshoe I
He was responsible for uniting a coalition of peoples into the Basotho nation.

Royal visit
This stamp marks the visit of King George VI to Basutoland in 1947.

Kingdom of Lesotho
Ths stamp, issued in 1966, celebrates recent independent status.

© DIAGRAM

Liberia

In 1816, the American Colonization Society founded Monrovia, now capital of Liberia, as a home for freed slaves. Liberia declared its independence on July 26, 1847. The new country faced many economic problems. But, in 1926, the economy improved when the government leased land to the American Firestone Tire and Rubber Company for rubber plantations. William Tubman, who became president in 1943, did not permit opposition, but he tried to involve the local people in politics alongside the Americo-Liberians, the descendants of freed slaves, who dominated the government. He also developed the interior, while foreign investment was attracted by his "open door" policy. Tubman died in 1971. His successor was another Americo-Liberian, William Tolbert, who faced economic problems. Prices rose and riots occurred in 1979.

In 1980, a military group composed of non-Americo-Liberians killed Tolbert and Master Sergeant Samuel Doe became head of state. Multiparty elections were held in 1985. Doe was elected president. Under Doe, many opposition leaders were killed or imprisoned. A rebellion, which broke out in late 1989, developed into civil war which continued until 1996. A peace-keeping force sent by the Economic Community of West African States (ECOWAS) tried to restore order. However, in September 1990, Doe was killed by rebel forces. ECOWAS installed a provisional government led by Amos Sawyer. Under Sawyer a series of ceasefires were agreed and broken. In 1995, Charles Taylor, one of the main rebel leaders, was invited to join the government. Taylor was elected president in 1997. Despite attempts to restore stability, a new rebel uprising occurred in the north in 1999. The rebels called themselves Liberians United for Reconciliation and Democracy.

Tribute
This Liberian stamp, issued in 1952, honors the United Nations.

Leaders

Doe, Samuel Kenyon
(1951–1990)
A member of the Krahn people, and a former army sergeant, Doe became president after a coup in 1980 in which President Tolbert was killed. He was elected president in 1985, despite charges of vote rigging. A civil war broke out in 1989 and, in 1990, Doe was captured by rebels, tortured and killed.

Taylor, Charles Ghankay
(1948–)
Taylor was born of a Liberian mother and American father. He joined Doe's government in the 1980s, but fled to the United States after being charged with embezzlement. He returned to Liberia to lead the rebel National Patriotic Front of Liberia. He joined the government in 1995 and, in 1997, he was elected president.

Tubman, William Vacanarat Shadrach
(1895–1971)
Tubman, an Americo-Liberian, served as president from 1944 until 1971. His "open-door" policies attracted foreign investment and reduced the dependence on aid from the United States. He was the first president to support the nation's indigenous people.

...eria timeline

...-19th century

1461 CE Portuguese merchants start to trade on the Grain Coast in what is now Liberia

...h century

1816 The American Colonization Society (ACS) buys land along the Grain Coast and founds Monrovia

1822 The ACS settles the first group of freed slaves at Monrovia

1847 **July 26** Liberia becomes independent. Joseph J Roberts, an American freed man born in Virginia, becomes president

...0–1949

1915 Uprising by the indigenous peoples against the Americo-Liberians

1926 Liberia leases land to the American Firestone Company

1943 William V. S. Tubman becomes President

...0–1969

1960 Liberia offers a "flag of convenience" to ship owners

...0–1979

1971 Tubman is succeeded as president by William R. Tolbert

1979 Increase in the price of rice causes rioting against Americo-Liberian political domination

...0–1989

1980 Tolbert is killed during a military coup: Master Sergeant Samuel K. Doe becomes president

1985 Doe and his National Democratic Party win multiparty elections amid allegations of vote rigging

1989 A former Doe supporter, Charles Taylor invades from Ivory Coast

...0–1999

1990 Full scale civil war breaks out between Doe's Armed Forces of Liberia (AFL) and two rebel groups, the Independent National Patriotic Front of Liberia (INPFL) and Taylor's National Patriotic Front of Liberia (NPFL)

1990 **Sept.** Doe is killed by the INPFL

1990 **Nov.** West African peacekeeping troops arrive to police a cease-fire

1993 A seven-month ceasefire is agreed

1995 Charles Taylor is brought into the transitional government

1996 The warring parties sign a peace agreement

1997 Presidential and legislative elections are held: Charles Taylor becomes president

1999 Fighting breaks out in the north where a group called Liberians United for Reconciliation and Democracy mounts a rebellion against Taylor's government

...0–

2000 The European Union suspends aid to Liberia following charges that Liberia is helping the rebels in Sierra Leone; Liberia accuses Guinea and Sierra Leone of supporting the rebels in northern Liberia

2001 UN Security Council imposes arms embargo to punish Taylor for trading weapons for diamonds from rebels in Sierra Leone

2002 Taylor declares a state of emergency

A common goal
Freedom from oppression is praised on Liberia's coat of arms.

Joseph Jenkins Roberts
An immigrant to Liberia, he served as president from 1847–1856.

National Day
Liberians celebrate the occasion with an emotive display of flags.

© DIAGRAM

Libya

Wind of change
This stamp, issued in 1978, marked International Anti-Apartheid Year.

A captured flag
Italy invaded Libya in 1911 after defeating Ottoman Turkey.

Libya became independent as a monarchy on December 24, 1951. Its king, who had been chosen by the national assembly in 1950, was Idri (Muhammad Idris al-Mahdi), a leader who had resisted Italian rule. Political parties were forbidden. In 1959, the discovery of oil transformed the economy, though most people remained poor, receivin little benefit from the oil bonanza. Discontent with the government led group of officers to overthrow the monarchy. They declared the count republic, which was called the Libyan Arab Republic. The new regim led by Colonel Muammar al-Quaddafi, was strongly Muslim and pro-Arab. It broke Libya's close ties with the West and sought to create unions with other Arab countries. But these unions did not last.

Quaddafi used money from oil sales to develop the economy. In 197 he set up local, regional and national congresses through which the people could express their views. However, despite this apparently democratic structure, the government did not permit political oppositi In 1977, Quaddafi declared Libya a one-party socialist *jamahariya*, a word meaning "state of the masses." In international affairs, Quaddafi supported radical movements. The US accused Libya of supporting international terrorism and, in 1986, broke all ties with Libya. After Libya fired missiles at US military aircraft in 1986, the US bombed military bases in Tripoli and Benghazi. In 1992, the UN imposed sanctions on Libya for refusing to hand over people suspected of attac on a Pan Am airliner in 1988 and a French airliner in 1989. In 1999, Quaddafi surrendered the two Libyans suspected of planting the bomb the airliner. As a result, the UN lifted many of its sanctions. In 2002 Quaddafi announced his detention of two al Qaida suspects.

Leaders

Idris I
(1890–1983)
Idris became king in 1951 when the country became independent. The National Assembly had chosen him to fill this role in 1950. He had earlier served as Emir of Cyrenaica, one of three provinces which made up Libya. He had also led resistance to Italian rule and, in 1969, was deposed by a group of army officers.

Quaddafi, Muammar al-
(1942–)
Muammar al-Quaddafi became leader of Libya, and commander-of-chief of the armed forces, in 1969 after a group of army officers had overthrown Idris I. At home, Quaddafi reorganized Libyan society along socialist, nationalist lines. Abroad, he supported radical groups, including the Black Panthers in the United States and the Irish Republican Army

(IRA) in Northern Ireland. As a result, he became a controversi figure. In 1986, US planes bomb several sites in Libya, but Quaddafi was not harmed. In th late 1990s and early 2000s, Quaddafi sought to restore goo relations with other countries. In 2001, he stated that he wished normalize relations with the Unit States and he described the terorist attacks on September 1 as "horrifying."

ya timeline

th century BCE	Phoenician settlements founded on the Libyan coast
th century BCE	Tripolitania is part of the Carthaginian empire: Cyrenaica (eastern Libya) comes under Greek control
146 BCE	Tripolitania becomes part of the Roman empire
96 BCE	Cyrenaica becomes part of the Roman empire
643–647 CE	Libya is conquered by the Islamic Arabs
868–972	Libya is independent under the Tulunid dynasty
990–1171	Libya is part of the Fatimid caliphate of Cairo
1551	Libya is conquered by the Ottoman Turks
1711	Libya becomes autonomous under the Qaramanli dynasty

h century

1804	US navy attacks a base of the Barbary Corsairs at Tripoli
1835	Direct Ottoman rule is restored

0–1949

1912	The Ottomans cede Libya to Italy
1923	The Italians gain control over Tripolitania (northwest Libya)
1931	The Italians gain full control over Cyrenaica
1940	The Italians invade Egypt from Libya
1943	The British drive the Italians and Germans out of Libya, and set up an Allied military government
1947	Italy abandons its claims to Libya

0–1959

1951	**Dec. 24** Libya becomes an independent kingdom of three federated provinces under King Idris I
1954	Idris grants the US military and naval bases in Libya

0–1969

1963	The provinces are abolished as Libya becomes a unitary state
1969	King Idris is overthrown by a military coup: Col. Muammar al-Quaddafi becomes head of state

0–1979

1973	Quaddafi sets up a system of local, regional and national popularly elected congresses
1977	Quaddafi declares Libya a one-party socialist *jamahiriya* ("state of the masses")

0–1989

1980	Quaddafi proposes a union between Libya and Chad
1981	US shoots down two Libyan jets over the Gulf of Sirte
1986	US aircraft bomb Tripoli and Benghazi in response to Libyan support for international terrorism
1989	Libya joins the Arab Maghreb Union

0–1999

1992	UN sanctions imposed on Libya after it refuses to hand over two agents suspected of the 1988 Pan Am Flight 103 bombing over Lockerbie, Scotland
1993	UN tightens sanctions against Libya
1999	Libya hands over the two Libyans suspected of bombing the Pan Am flight over Scotland in 1988

0–

2000	Libya helps to secure the release of hostages held by Muslim rebels in the Philippines
2002	Despite Quaddafi's condemnation of the September 11 bombings, Libya remains one of the seven countries blacklisted by the US for supporting terrorism

Italian supremacy
This stamp, issued in 1921, celebrated the dominance of Italy over Libya at that time.

An Allied victory
The Italian and German forces were driven out of Libya by the Allied forces in 1943.

Air strikes against Libya
On 15 April, 1986, the US air force attacked targets near the harbor in Tripoli in retaliation for suspected acts of terrorism by Libya.

© DIAGRAM

Malawi

In 1891, Britain made the area which now forms Malawi a protectorate (colony) called Nyasaland. In 1953, Britain linked Nyasaland with Northern and Southern Rhodesia (now Zambia and Zimbabwe) in the Federation of Rhodesia and Nyasaland. Nationalists in all the territories opposed the creation of the federation, fearing political domination and racial discrimination by the white minority. In Malawi, Dr Hastings Kamuzu Banda led the opposition to the federation. In 1958, a state of emergency was declared. Opposition leaders, including Banda, were arrested. Their party, the Nyasaland Congress Party, was banned. Banda was released in 1960, and the renamed Malawi Congress Party (MCP) won elections in 1961. Nyasaland became independent as Malawi on July 6, 1964. Malawi became a republic in 1966 and Banda became president of the one-party nation. In 1971, he was proclaimed "president for life."

Banda maintained close contacts with the white-dominated countries southern Africa, a policy largely dictated by Malawi's geographical position, and the economy thrived as the country attracted foreign investment. But Banda's rule became increasingly autocratic and his government was criticized for its abuses of human rights. Malawi held first parliamentary elections since independence in 1978. Other elections were held in 1983, 1987, and 1992. However, all the candidates belong to the MCP, the sole political party. In the early 1990s, the government was beset by economic problems, drought and harvest failures. In 199 the people voted to restore a multiparty system. Banda's title "president for life" was withdrawn, and he was defeated in presidential elections 1994. The victor was Bakili Muluzi, who was reelected in 1999.

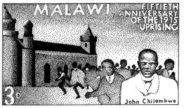

Uprising
A 1965 stamp commemorates the 50th anniversary of the uprising led by John Chilembwe against cruelty on colonial farms.

Leaders

Banda, Dr Hastings Kamuzu
(1902–1997)
Hasting Kamuzu Banda became Malawi's prime minister in 1963 and president in 1966. He encouraged private enterprise, unlike some of his socialist neighbors. He became "president for life" in 1971, but his title was withdrawn in 1993 when multiparty rule was restored. He lost the 1994 elections to Muluzi.

Chilembwe, John
(c.1860–1915)
A Baptist minister, John Chilembwe studied theology in the United States. He later founded the Province Industrial Mission at Mbombwe, Nyasaland, in 1900. In 1915, he led an uprising against British rule. His action was in response to the cruelty of some white plantation owners. His uprising failed. He was arrested and shot.

Muluzi, Bakili
(1943–)
In 1994, following the adoption multiparty constitution in Malawi Muluzi stood as the opposition candidate to President Banda i the presidential elections. He defeated Banda and two other candidates and became president. He was reelected in 1999. Muluzi became leader of the United Democratic Front in 1992.

awi timeline

15th century	The Maravi (Malawi) kingdom dominates the Malawi region
17th century	The Portuguese are the first Europeans to explore the region

h century

1830s CE	Ngoni and Yao peoples settle in the area of present-day Malawi
1859	The British missionary David Livingstone visits the region and finds it torn by civil wars
1875	The Free Church of Scotland sets up a mission station
1889	The British make protection treaties with local chiefs
1891	The British proclaim the Protectorate of Nyasaland

)0–1949

1915	John Chilembwe leads an unsuccessful rebellion against British rule in which he is killed
1944	The Nyasaland African Congress, the first national political movement, holds its first assembly

i0–1959

1958	Hastings Kamuzu Banda becomes leader of the Nyasaland independence movement, the Malawi Congress Party (MCP)

i0–1969

1964	**Jul 6** Nyasaland becomes independent as Malawi: Banda becomes prime minister
1966	Malawi becomes a one-party state: Banda becomes president

i0–1979

1970	Banda becomes president for life

i0–1999

1993	Banda gives up the life presidency and prepares to hold elections
1994	Bakili Muluzi of the United Democratic Front Party becomes president after defeating Banda in multiparty elections
1995	Banda is acquitted on charges of conspiracy to murder four opposition politicians in 1983
1997	Following his death, Banda is given a state funeral
1999	Muluzi is reelected president

i0–

2000	Muluzi dismisses his entire cabinet following charges of corruption
2001	Six people are charged with treason because of their alleged involvement in a plot to overthrow the government
2002	Muluzi accepts parliament's ruling that the number of presidential terms be limited to two

A former colony
This stamp was issued in 1897, a time when Nyasaland (now known as Malawi) was still part of British Central Africa.

© DIAGRAM

Mali

French influence in what is now Mali began in the mid-nineteenth century. But France did not win control over the area until 1895. In 19[?] Mali, then known as French Sudan, became part of French West Afric[?] which also included what are now Benin, Burkina Faso, Guinea, Ivory Coast, Mauritania, Niger, and Senegal. In 1946, French Sudan became French overseas territory and, in 1958, it became a self-governing member of the French Union called the Sudanese Republic. In 1959, t[?] Sudanese Republic and Senegal set up a federation called Mali. This federation broke up in 1960. The Sudanese Republic then became full[?] independent as the Republic of Mali on June 20, 1960. In 1964, the fir[?] president, Modibo Keita, made Mali a one-party state. Links were established with the Communist world and Mali obtained little Wester[?] aid. In 1968, the arrest of some army officers by the People's Militia le[?] the army to intervene and Keita was overthrown in a bloodless coup.

An independent nation
This is a stamp, issued in 1960, which marks Mali's newly-acquired independent status and acceptance into the United Nations.

The new head of state, Moussa Traoré, aimed at restoring the countr[?] economy, but droughts in the 1970s made progress difficult. In 1974, t[?] people voted for the creation of a National Assembly and a president elected on a one-party basis. Elections were held in 1979 and Traoré w[?] elected president. His government consisted of civilians, but the milita[?] remained powerful. In 1991, a military group led by Ahmadou Toure deposed Traoré and a constitution permitting multiparty elections was adopted. In 1992, an opposition leader, Alpha Oumar Konaré, became Mali's first democratically elected president. His party, the Alliance fo[?] Democracy in Mali (ADEMA) won a majority in the National Assem[?] Traoré was reelected in 1996, but he stood down in 2002. Ahmadou Toure was elected president.

Leaders

Keita, Modibo
(1915–1977)
Modibo Keita became president of the Mali Federation, consisting of Senegal and the Sudanese Republic (French Sudan). This federation broke up in 1969 and Keita became president of Mali, as the Sudanese Republic was renamed. He made Mali a one-party state, but was deposed by a coup led by Moussa Traoré in 1968.

Konaré, Alpha Oumar
(1946–)
Alpha Konaré was elected president of Mali in 1992 following a period of military rule. He was reelected in 1997. In 2001, Konaré cancelled a referendum that would give the president immunity from prosecution. He retired in 2002, having served the maximum of two full terms as president. Konaré was a former teacher and writer.

Traoré, Moussa
(1936–)
Moussa Traoré became head o[?] state in 1968 after leading a cou[?] that deposed Modibo Keita. He[?] was deposed by another coup [?] 1991 led by Ahmadou Toure, w[?] restored democracy in 1992. In [?] 1999, Traoré was sentenced to death on corruption charges, but his sentence was commuted to life imprisonment.

timeline

-19th century

c. 400 CE	The earliest city in sub-Saharan Africa develops at Jenne-jeno
c. 700–1205	Western Mali region dominated by the Ghana empire
c. 1000	Islam introduced into the Mali region by Arab and Berber merchants
c. 1240–1450	The empire of Mali is the dominant West African power
1312–1337	Timbuktu becomes a major center of Islamic culture under King Mansa Musa
c. 1450–1591	The Songhay empire dominates the Mali region
1493–1528	Songhay empire at its peak under Askia Muhammad
1591	Morocco destroys the Songhay empire

h century

1850	Mali area conquered by the Islamic reformer al-Hajj Umar of the Tukolor caliphate
1866	The French begin the conquest of Mali
1895	France wins full control of Mali: it becomes the colony of French Sudan

0–1949

1904	The French Sudan, renamed the Sudanese Republic, is incorporated into the French West Africa colony
1946	The Sudanese Republic is given a legislative council

0–1959

1958	The Sudanese Republic gains full internal self-government
1959	The Sudanese Republic and Senegal merge to form the Federation of Mali

0–1969

1960 Jun 20	The Federation of Mali becomes independent
1960 Aug 20	Senegal leaves the federation
1960 Sept 22	The independent Republic of Mali is proclaimed: Modibo Keita is the first president
1968	Keita is overthrown by a military coup. Gen. Moussa Traoré becomes head of government

0–1979

1974	Traoré makes Mali a one-party state

0–1999

1991	Traoré is overthrown by a military coup: a transitional military-civilian government is created
1992	Alpha Oumar Konaré becomes president in elections under a new multiparty constitution
1993	An attempted coup to restore Traoré is defeated
1997	Konaré is re-elected president

0–

2000	The World Bank and the International Monetary Fund (IMF) agree to reduce Mali's international debts
2002	Konaré retires after serving the maximum two terms and Ahmadou Toure is elected president

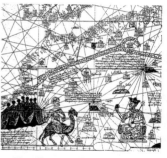

Trading partners (above)
The king of Mali (bottom right) offers a gold nugget to the Arab merchant approaching him (bottom left) on a map dating from the 14th century.

Enslaved
This is a wooden sculpture of a man with both hands and feet tightly bound, which was made by the Dogon people of modern Mali.

© DIAGRAM

Mauritania

France began to take control of what is now Mauritania in the mid-19 century. Finally, in 1902, it declared the area a French protectorate (colony). In 1920, it became part of French West Africa, which also included what are now Benin, Burkina Faso, Guinea, Ivory Coast, Ma Niger, and Senegal. Mauritania became a separate territory in the Fre Union in 1946 and it finally won its independence on November 28, 1960. At first, Morocco refused to recognize Mauritania, because it claimed that, historically, Mauritania was part of Morocco. But Morocco's King Hassan II recognized Mauritania's independence in 1969. Mauritania's first president, Moktar Ould Daddah, set up a one-party system in 1964. In 1968, he made Arabic the official language, though many black African peoples in the south feared Arab dominat In foreign affairs, Ould Daddah adopted an anti-Western stance.

In 1974, Morocco announced that it would take over Spanish (now Western) Sahara. Mauritania also asserted its claim to this territory. In 1975, Spain negotiated a plan to partition the territory when it withdre in 1976. Mauritanian troops occupied the southern third of Western Sahara, but guerrilla forces of Polisario (Popular Front for the Liberat of Saharan Territories) opposed Mauritania. The war was a drain on t economy and, in 1979, Mauritania withdrew. Morocco then occupied entire territory. In 1978, Ould Daddah was deposed in a coup and a military regime ruled the country. In 1984, after a period of uncertaint Maaouiya Ould Sidi Ahmed Taya, an army colonel, seized power. In 1991, Mauritania restored multiparty democracy. In 1992, Taya was elected president. He was reelected in 1997. Severe drought affected Mauritania in 2002, causing famine.

Republican flag
This is a stamp issued in 1960 to mark the inauguration of an Islamic Republic in Mauritania.

Leaders

Haidalla, Mohammed Khouna Ould
(1940–)
Haidalla became prime minister and chief of the ruling military council which took over the government of Mauritania after Moktar Ould Daddah was deposed in 1978. He proclaimed himself president in 1980, but he was deposed in 1984 by Colonel Maaouiya Ould Sidi Ahmed Taya.

Ould Daddah, Moktar
(1924–)
Moktar Ould Daddah became the first president of Mauritania in 1960 and held office until 1978. He tried to unite his ethnically diverse people. But Mauritania's unsuccessful attempt to take over the southern third of Western (formerly Spanish) Sahara led to a decline in his popularity and his downfall in a coup.

Taya, Maaouiya Ould Sidi Ahmed
(1943–)
Colonel Taya took power in 198 and led a military government. Under a new constitution introduced in 1991, he was elected president of in 1992 an reelected in 1997. Taya served the war in Western Sahara between 1976 and 1978. He served as prime minister and minister of defense under Haida

ritania timeline

-19th century

c. 700–1205 CE	Southern Mauritania region dominated by the Ghana empire
c. 1000	Islam introduced into the Mauritania region by Arab and Berber merchants
1448	The Portuguese establish a trading post on the coast of Mauritania
c. 1450–1591	The Songhay empire dominates much of Mauritania region
1591	Mauritania is conquered by Morocco

n century

1858	France begins to extend military control over southern Mauritania
1898	Xavier Coppolani wins the Berber tribes of southern Mauritania over to French rule

0–1949
1902	French authority is effective in most of Mauritania
1920	Mauritania becomes a French colony
1946	Mauritania becomes a territory of the French Union with a legislative council

0–1959
1955	The Rigaibat are the last Mauritanian tribe to be pacified
1958	Mauritania is granted powers of internal self-government
1959	Mokhtar Ould Daddah becomes prime minister of Mauritania

0–1969
1960 Nov 28	Mauritania becomes independent
1961	Ould Daddah is elected as the first president of Mauritania
1965	Mauritania becomes a one-party state

0–1979
1976	Mauritania and Morocco take over administration of Western Sahara (formerly Spanish Sahara)
1978	Ould Daddah is overthrown by a military coup
1979	Mauritania gives up its claim to Western Sahara and withdraws

0–1989
1980	After a long period of political uncertainty, Muhammad Ould Haidalla becomes head of government
1984	Col. Maawiya Ould Taya becomes president in a bloodless coup
1989	Inter-ethnic violence breaks out on the border with Senegal

0–1999
1991	Taya introduces a multiparty constitution
1992	Maaouiya Ould Taya is elected president in the first elections under the new constitution
1997	Taya is reelected president

0–
2000	The offshore fishing industry continues to suffer because of competition with foreign fishing fleets
2001	Muhammad VI of Morocco visits Mauritania, indicating the importance both countries attach to improving relations

Handing over control
In 1958 Mauritania became a self-governing colony within the French Union. Its first prime minister, Moktar Ould Daddah (left), is shown here with General Charles De Gaulle of France (right).

Reunited
This is a stamp issued in 1976 to mark the reunification of Western Sahara with Mauritania.

Morocco

French Morocco became independent on March 2, 1956. Spain, which ruled the rest of the country, then gave up its claims except for two small areas on the north coast, called Ceuta and Melilla. The port of Tangier, which had been under international control, became part of Morocco in October 1956. In 1957, Sultan Muhammad V, who had been exiled for demanding his country's independence, changed his title to King Muhammad. When Muhammad died in 1961, he was succeeded by his son, who became King Hassan II. In 1965, Hassan dissolved parliament but, in 1970, Morocco adopted a new constitution, restoring a degree of parliamentary government. Despite several attempts on his life, Hassan carried out reforms. In 1977, the country became a constitutional monarchy with an elected parliament.

In 1976, Spain withdrew from Spanish (now Western) Sahara, a desert territory between Morocco and Mauritania. With Spain's agreement, Morocco occupied the northern two-thirds of the territory, while Mauritania took the rest. But the people of Western Sahara formed a guerrilla force, called Polisario (Popular Front for the Liberation of Saharan Territories). Polisario fought against the Moroccans and Mauritanians. In 1979, Mauritania withdrew and Morocco occupied the entire territory. After the fighting ended in 1991, Polisario continued to demand independence. United Nations attempts to hold a vote on the territory's future failed, because it could not draw up a voters' list acceptable to both Polisario and Morocco. When Hassan died in 1999, was succeeded by his son, King Muhammad VI. Muhammad was thought to be a reformer, but he was also expected to follow the same cautious approach to Morocco's many problems as his father.

Give peace a chance
In June 2002 women and children were caught up in the debate about the liberation of the Saharan territories from Moroccan control.

Leaders

Muhammad V
(1909–1961)
Muhammad V served as sultan of Morocco from 1927–1957, and as king from 1957 until his death. He became involved in nationalist politics in 1943 and, during 1953–1955, he was exiled by the French. Following independence in 1956, he worked hard to make Morocco a constitutional monarchy.

Hassan II
(1929–1999)
Hassan II served as king from 1961 until his death in 1999. He worked towards making his country a constitutional monarchy. In 1972, he became chairman of the Organization of African Unity (OAU). However, Morocco withdrew from the OAU in 1985, when Polisario rebels from Western Sahara were admitted to the organization.

Muhammad VI
(1963–)
Muhammad VI is the oldest son Hassan II of Morocco. Born in Rabat, he was given the title Crown Prince Sidi Muhammad. became King Muhammad VI on the death of his father in 1999. Educated mainly in Morocco and France, he was thought to favor reformist policies, including the extension of women's rights.

occo timeline

475–450 BCE	Carthaginians establish colonies on the Moroccan coast
40–44 CE	Morocco becomes part of the Roman empire
702	The Berbers of Morocco submit to the Arabs and accept Islam
788	Idris I Ibn Abdullah breaks away from the Arab caliphate and founds an independent Idrisid caliphate of Morocco
926	The Idrisid caliphate is conquered by the Umayyad emirate of Cordoba
1056	Yusuf Ibn Tashfin founds the Sanhaja Berber Almoravid emirate in southern Morocco
1147	The Almohad dynasty replaces the Almoravids
1269	The Marinid dynasty overthrows the Almohads
1465	The Wattasid dynasty succeeds the Marinids in Morocco
1554	The Saadi dynasty replaces the Wattasids
1591	Saadi sultan Ahmed al-Mansur captures Timbuktu
1666	Moulay al-Rashid is proclaimed sultan, founding the Alawi dynasty (still in power 2002)

h century

1844	French defeat the Moroccans at Isly
1894	Tribal rebellion in the Rif provokes a Spanish invasion
00–1949 CE 1904	Franco-Spanish treaty grants Spain sphere of influence in northern Morocco
1912 Mar.	Treaty of Fez; Morocco becomes a French protectorate
1921–1926	Rebellion of Abd el-Krim in the Rif Atlas
1940 Jun.	Morocco comes under control of the collaborationist Vichy government following the fall of France in World War II
1942 Nov.	Operation Torch: Anglo-American landings in Morocco
1944	The Istiqlal (Independence) party is founded
50–1959 1953	France deposes the nationalist sultan Muhammad V
1956 Mar. 2	Morocco becomes independent: Muhammad V is restored
1956 Apr.	Spanish zone (except Ceuta and Melilla) and Tangier are restored to Morocco
1957	Muhammad V exchanges the title of sultan for king
60–1969 1961	Death of Muhammad V: succeeded by his son, Hassan II
1965	Riots in Casablanca lead King Hassan to assume direct rule
70–1979 1976	On Spanish withdrawal, Morocco and Mauritania partition Western Sahara (formerly Spanish Sahara)
1979	Morocco claims sovereignty over all of Western Sahara and builds a fortified wall through it
80–1989 1989	Morocco joins other N. African states in Arab Maghrib Union
90–1999 1991 Sept.	Ceasefire between Morocco and Polisario in Western Sahara
1999 Jul. 23	King Hassan II dies: succeeded by his son, Sidi Muhammad, who becomes Muhammad VI
00– 2002	The UN's Western Sahara Mission is extended through January 2003

Invaders
Muslims from North Africa conquered Southern Spain by sea between 700–1200.

Algeçiras, Spain, 1906
Moroccan delegates attended a conference to debate future control of their country.

Resistance fighter
Abd al Krim, founder of the 1921–1926 Republic of the Rif.

© DIAGRAM

65

Mozambique

In 1950, Portugal gave its colony of Mozambique overseas province status. However, in 1960, a guerrilla force, called FRELIMO (Front for the Liberation of Mozambique) was formed in Mozambique. By 1964 FRELIMO controlled part of northern Mozambique. After a coup occurred in Portugal in 1974, the new government agreed to the independence of Mozambique. This was achieved on June 25, 1975. Samora Machel, FRELIMO's leader, then made his country a one-par Marxist state. He also provided a base for ZANU (Zimbabwe African National Union) guerrillas. In return, Rhodesian and South African forces attacked Mozambique. In 1980 Mozambique helped exiled members of the ANC (African National Congress). In retaliation, Sou Africa supported a guerrilla force, called RENAMO (National Resistance Movement), to fight against the Mozambique government. The war that followed shattered the economy.

In 1986, Machel was killed in a plane crash and Joaquim Chissano became president. The government finally ended its Marxist policies i 1989. In 1990, the government legalized opposition parties, provided f secret elections, and introduced a bill of rights. In 1992, FRELIMO an RENAMO signed a peace agreement, ending 16 years of civil war. Th country's first multiparty elections held in 1994 were won by FRELIM while Chissano defeated his RENAMO opponent Afonso Dhlakama i presidential elections. During the 1990s, the government followed the free market policies advocated by the IMF (International Monetary Fund) and rebuilt its economy. By 1999, Mozambique's economy was rated as the fastest growing in the world. But severe floods in 2000 caused a major disaster.

FRELIMO
This is a poster publicizing the Front for the Liberation of Mozambique, which created a one-party, Marxist state there.

Leaders

Chissano, Joaquim Alberto
(1939–)
Chissano became prime minister in 1974 and president in 1986, when Samora Machel was killed in a plane crash. Chissano had been a colleague of Machel during the guerrilla struggle against Portuguese colonial rule. He restored peace and democracy in Mozambique, and was reelected in 1994 and 1999.

Dhlakama, Afonso Marceta Macacho
(1953–)
Dhlakama became president of RENAMO (National Resistance Movement) in 1982, a guerrilla group which had been formed in 1976 with Rhodesian and, later, South African support. He was a member of FRELIMO, during the struggle for independence.

Machel, Samora Moises
(1933–1986)
Machel became the first preside of Mozambique when the countr won its independence in 1975. I had been active in the anticolon struggle and was president of FRELIMO. In office, he followed Marxist-Leninist policies and supported equal-rights movements in Rhodesia (Zimbabwe) and South Africa.

zambique timeline

3rd century CE	Bantu-speaking herders and ironworkers move into the Mozambique region
14th century	Swahili merchants found trading cities at Sofala and Chibuene
1508	The Portuguese found the city of Moçambique
1531	The Portuguese begin to extend their control inland along the Zambesi River

th century

1833	Shoshangane of the Nguni massacres the garrison of Lourenço Marques (now Maputo)
1836	Shoshangane burns Sofala
1859	Death of Shoshangane

00–1949

1921	Portugal introduces the *assimilado* system, which enables some Africans to attain Portuguese citizenship
1930	Colonial Act encourages emigration to Mozambique

50–1959

1951	Mozambique becomes an overseas province of Portugal

60–1969

1961	Front for the Liberation of Mozambique (FRELIMO) guerrilla movement founded to fight for independence
1964	FRELIMO gains control of northern Mozambique
1969	The moderate president Mondlane of FRELIMO is assassinated: he is replaced by the Marxist Samora Machel

70–1979

1974	Portugal agrees to grant independence to Mozambique
1975 Jun 25	Mozambique becomes independent: Samora Machel becomes president
1976	Mozambique closes its border with Rhodesia (now Zimbabwe). Rhodesia forms the Mozambique National Resistance (RENAMO) to undermine the FRELIMO regime

80–1989

1980	South Africa begins supporting RENAMO after the white government of Rhodesia falls
1984	Mozambique and South Africa sign a non-aggression pact
1986	President Machel is killed in a plane crash, Joaquim Chissano becomes president
1989	Mozambique officially renounces Marxist policies

090–1999

1990	Ban on opposition parties lifted
1992	FRELIMO and RENAMO sign a peace agreement
1994	FRELIMO leader Joaquim Chissano wins the first multiparty presidential elections
1995	Mozambique joins the Commonwealth of Nations
1996	Mozambique joins the Community of Portuguese-speaking Countries

000–

2000	Central and southern Mozambique devastated by floods caused by the worst rain in 40 years; one third of the country's corn crop is destroyed
2001	The Health Ministry announces that one in five pregnant women is infected by the HIV/AIDS virus
2002	Sharp rise in malaria rates is attributed to the fact that the waters of the floods in 2000 have yet to drain away

Liberation
This is a typical freedom fighter caught up in the struggle against colonial rule in Mozambique.

Revolution
FRELIMO guerrillas welcomed by Mozambicans.

MOCAMBIQUE
INDEPENDENCIA DO ZIMBABWE 18•4•80
10$00

Independence
This 1980 stamp marks Zimbabwe's change in status.

© DIAGRAM

67

Namibia

In World War I, South African troops conquered German Southwest Africa (now Namibia). In 1920, the League of Nations mandated South Africa to rule this former German colony. In 1960, the South West Afri People's Organization (SWAPO) became the chief nationalist group opposing South African rule and, in 1966, it began a guerrilla war. In 1968, at SWAPO's request, the United Nations renamed the territory Namibia. In 1971, the International Court of Justice declared that Sout Africa's rule of Namibia was illegal. In the late 1980s, fierce fighting between South African troops and SWAPO guerrillas led South Africa agree a ceasefire. Elections in 1989 were won by SWAPO. In February 1990, the Assembly voted for a new constitution. It provided for elections of a president who would serve two five-year terms and an elected parliament consisting of two houses. Sam Nujoma, the SWAPC leader, became president. His broad-based government included whites

Namibia became independent on March 21, 1990. In 1994, South Africa, which had ruled the small but economically important Walvis Bay since 1910, returned the area to Namibia. Nujoma was reelected president in 1994 but, in 1998, he was criticized for his autocratic style and also for sending Namibian troops to support the government of the Democratic Republic of Congo (formerly Zaïre) in a civil war. But afte Namibia's constitution was changed to allow the president a third term office, Nujoma was reelected by a large majority in 1999. In 1999, a separatist group in the Caprivi Strip rebelled, demanding independence for the Strip, which is populated by Lozi people, who live mainly in Zambia. Government troops soon put down the rebellion. Nujoma supported Robert Mugabe's land seizures in 2002.

Independence
A billboard poster, situated in Windhoek, Namibia, captures the mood of celebration upon independence.

Leaders

Kutako, Chief Hosea
(1870–1970)
Chief of the Herero people of South West Africa (now Namibia), Kutako opposed German colonization and South African rule. Wounded in the Herero revolt of 1904–1905), when around three-quarters of the Herero people were killed or driven into exile. He regularly petitioned the UN for independence in the 1950s.

Nujoma, Sam Daniel
(1929–)
Nujoma founded the South West African People's Organization (SWAPO) in 1960. From 1966, he led SWAPO in a guerrilla war against the South African occupation of the territory. Nujoma became president of Namibia when it became independent in 1990, and was reelected in 1994 and 1999.

Toivo, ja Toivo, Animba Herma
(1924–)
Leader of the Ovamboland People's Organization, which opposed apartheid in Namibia in 1959, Toivo helped to found the South West African People's Organization (SWAPO). He serve 16 years imprisonment on Robben Island, South Africa, and later became secretary-general of SWAPO.

nibia timeline

15th century		Bantu-speaking peoples migrate into the Namibia region
	1485 CE	Portuguese navigator Diogo Cão arrives at Cape Cross
h century		
	1870	Germans make peace agreements with local chiefs
	1876	Britain annexes Walvis Bay
	1884	Germany creates the German Southwest Africa colony
	1894	Chief Hendrik Witbooi is killed leading a joint Nama-Herero rebellion against the Germans
00–1949	**1904**	The Herero rebel once more against German rule
	1907	The Germans crush the Herero rebellion
	1910	Walvis Bay becomes part of South Africa
	1915	South African troops occupy German Southwest Africa in World War I
	1920	The League of Nations mandates Southwest Africa to South Africa
	1945	South Africa refuses a request to place Southwest Africa under UN trusteeship
	1946	The UN refuses to permit annexation of Southwest Africa by South Africa
	1948	South Africa's apartheid policies introduced into Southwest Africa
50–1959	**1958**	The Ovamboland People's Organization is founded
60–1969	**1960**	The Ovamboland People's Organization changes its name to South West Africa People's Organization (SWAPO)
	1966	The UN votes to end South Africa's mandate in Southwest Africa. SWAPO begins a guerrilla war for independence
	1968	At SWAPO's request, the UN changes the name of Southwest Africa to Namibia
	1969	South Africa ignores a UN ultimatum to withdraw from Namibia
70–1979	**1971**	The International Court of Justice declares South Africa's occupation of Southwest Africa to be illegal
	1973	UN recognizes SWAPO as the legitimate representative of the Namibians
	1975	SWAPO sets up bases in Angola
	1977	South Africa announces a plan to make Namibia independent under a white dominated government
	1978	SWAPO boycotts South African organized elections
80–1989	**1988**	After victories by Angolan-led SWAPO forces, South Africa agrees to make Namibia independent by 1990
90–1999	**1990**	**Mar 21** Namibia becomes independent: Sam Nujoma, the leader of SWAPO, becomes the first president
	1994	South Africa cedes Walvis Bay to Namibia
	1999	Nujoma is reelected president. Fighting erupts in the Caprivi Strip as separatist guerrillas clash with Namibian troops
00–	**2001**	The discovery of an offshore diamond-rich area sends mining companies flocking to Namibia

An oath of allegiance
Boer soldiers unite with the German Army in 1904–1907 to defeat the peoples of what was to become Namibia.

A German legacy
Herero women adopted the clothing style of the German missionaries who came to Namibia in the 19th century.

SWAPO
This is the insignia of the organization which led the resistance to the occupation of Namibia by South Africa.

© DIAGRAM

Niger

The French began to take over what is now Niger in 1891. They controlled most of the land by 1900, but had to put down Tuareg resistance in the north in the early 1900s. In 1922, France made Niger part of French West Africa, which also included what are now Benin, Burkina Faso, Guinea, Ivory Coast, Mali, Mauritania, and Senegal. In 1946, Niger became a French overseas territory and, in 1958, it became self-governing country in the French Community. Independence was achieved on August 3, 1960. Hamani Diori, Niger's first president, was skilled in foreign affairs, but the economy declined. When droughts hit Niger in the late 1960s and early 1970s, officials took much of the foreign aid for themselves. In 1974, Diori was overthrown in a coup.

The new head of state, Colonel Seyni Kountché, began to develop agriculture. He also set up a company, with 66 percent French capital, mine the country's uranium deposits. Uranium soon became Niger's chief export. Kountché died in 1987. His successor, Colonel Ali Saibou founded a new party, the National Movement for the Developing Socie (MNSD). The MNSD was meant to be the sole party. But in 1991, a national conference of political groups drew up a new constitution providing for multiparty elections. In 1992, Tuareg separatists launched rebellion in the north. In 1993, the victor in presidential elections was Mahamane Ousmane. His government signed a peace agreement with the Tuaregs in 1995, though one rebel group continued fighting until 1997. In 1996, Colonel Ibrahim Mainassara overthrew Ousmane and, later that year, he was elected president. After he was killed in 1999, Major Daouda Wanké became head of state. But multiparty rule was restored and Tandja Mamadou of the MNSD, was elected president.

A French West Africa colony
This stamp, issued between 1926–1940, shows a traditional craft on the River Niger.

Leaders

Diori, Hamani
(1916–1989)
Diori became president when Niger became independent in 1960. After an assassination attempt in 1963, he repressed criticism of his government. When Niger was hit by drought, his regime was accused of corruption. He was overthrown in 1974 and imprisoned from 1980 until 1984.

Kountché, Seyni
(1931–1987)
Kountché became Niger's first military leader in 1974, following the overthrow of President Hamani. He served as head of state until his death in 1987. He worked to restore an economy shattered by droughts and corruption. He included civilians in his government but did nothing to restore democracy.

Mamadou, Tandja
(1938–)
Mamadou was elected president of Niger in 1999. A retired lieutenant-colonel, he took part in the coup that overthrew President Hamani Diori in 1974 and he later served in government as interior minister. He ran for president against Mahamane Ousmane in 1996 and Ibrahim Mainassara in 1966.

er timeline

19th century

c. 1000 CE	Tuareg nomads migrate to the Niger region
14th century	Eastern Niger becomes part of the Kanem-Bornu empire
15th century	The Tuareg state of Aïr develops around Agadez. Western Niger becomes part of the Songhay empire
1515	Aïr is conquered by Askia Muhammad of the Songhay empire
1591	Aïr recovers its independence when Songhay is conquered by Morocco
18th century	The Hausa expand into Niger from the south

h century

1804	Hausa refugees from the Fulani *jihad* flood into Niger
1891	The French begin the conquest of Niger
1898	An Anglo-French commission demarcates the border between Niger and Nigeria

0–1949
1906	The French conquer Aïr. Niger's borders are demarcated
1917	The French expel most of the Tuareg from Niger after a rebellion
1922	Niger is incorporated into the French West Africa colony
1946	The *Parti Progressiste Nigérien* (PPN) is formed by Diori

0–1959
1958	Niger votes to retain links with France

0–1969
1960 Aug. 3	Niger becomes independent: Diori becomes the first president
1968–1973	A long drought devastates agriculture

0–1979
1971	Uranium mining begins in Niger
1974	Military coup ousts Diori: Seyni Kountché becomes president

0–1989
1984	Nigeria closes its borders with Niger causing economic hardship
1986	Nigeria re-opens its borders
1987	On the death of Kountché, Col. Ali Saibou becomes president
1989	Saibou is elected president. He is the only candidate

0–1999
1991	A national conference strips Saibou of his powers
1992	Niger adopts a multiparty constitution. A Tuareg rebellion breaks out in the north
1993	Mahamane Ousmane is elected president under the new constitution
1994	The government offers the Tuareg a degree of internal autonomy in return for a cease-fire
1996	Military coup ousts Ousmane: Gen. Ibrahim Mainassara becomes president
1997	The government and the Tuareg sign a ceasefire in Algiers
1999	Mainassara is assassinated: Daouda Malem Wanké becomes president. In subsequent elections, Tandja Mamadou is elected president

0–
2000	Foreign aid to Niger is resumed following the return to civil rule
2002	Government forces put down an army rebellion in the southeast

Sultan Ahmadu
He was leader when Niger was under threat from France in 1891.

Colonel Borgnis-Desbordes
He was leader of the French forces in 1891.

Samori Touré
He resisted European colonialism in the 1890s.

©DIAGRAM

Nigeria

Lagos in what is now Nigeria became a British colony in 1861 and, gradually, Britain extended its control over the south of the region. By 1914, all of Nigeria was a British colony. Opposition to colonial rule w blunted because of differences between leaders of rival ethnic groups. Nigeria became independent on October 1, 1960. In order to give pow to the major ethnic groups, Nigeria was divided into three regions: the North, where the Muslim Hausa were the leading group; the West, hor of the Yoruba; and the East, where the Igbo (or Ibo) formed a majority 1963, Nigeria became a federal republic. In 1966, Nigeria's first prime minister was killed in a military coup. The new military leader was an Igbo, who abolished the federal system and appointed Igbos to high office. This led to rioting in the north. In 1966, General Gowon took power. In 1967, Gowon divided Nigeria into 12 states, but, in 1967, Colonel Ojukwu proclaimed the Eastern Region an independent repub called Biafra. Civil war ensued, but Biafra surrendered in January 197

Gowon was deposed in 1975. His successor was killed in 1976 and followed by General Olesegun Obasanjo, who ended military rule in 1979. But the elected president was deposed in 1983 and yet another military regime took power. A return to civilian rule was promised, bu after elections in 1993 were annulled, General Abacha seized power. After Abacha died in 1998, civilian rule was finally restored. Obasanj the former military leader, was elected president in 1999, by which tin Nigeria was divided into 36 states, plus the capital Abuja. Obasanjo faced problems in creating national unity. In the early 2000s, Christia Muslim clashes occurred when some northern states adopted *sharia* (Islamic law), while Hausa-Yoruba conflict occurred in the southwest

Independence
On 1 October, 1960, Nigeria became independent of Britain, a fact celebrated on this heraldic display.

Leaders

Abacha, Sanni
(1943–1998)
Sanni Abacha became the military leader of Nigeria in 1993 following the annulment of the national election results. He was accused of abusing human rights and of consistently postponing the return to democracy. But, after his death in 1998, his successor General Abubakar, pushed quickly ahead to restore civilian rule.

Balewa, Sir Abubakar Tafawa
(1912–1966)
Sir Abubakar Tafawa Balewa was elected Nigeria's first prime minister in 1959. A Muslim northerner, he was determined that the country would not be dominated by western-educated southerners. He was knighted after Nigeria became independent in 1960, but he was assassinated in a military coup in 1966.

Obasanjo, Olesegun
(1937–)
Lieutenant-General Olesegun Obasanjo became Nigeria's military head of state in 1976. E he restored civilian rule in 1979 1999, he was elected presiden leading his People's Democrat Party to power. A Yoruba, he retired from the army in 1979. He was imprisoned from 1995–1998 for allegedly plotting a coup.

eria timeline

n century

1861 CE	Britain annexes Lagos
1885	Britain declares the Oil Rivers Protectorate over SE Nigeria
1886	The Royal Africa Company establishes a protectorate over much of western Nigeria
1893	The Yoruba agree to accept a British protectorate

0–1949

1900	The British government buys out the Royal Africa Company
1902	Britain conquers the Ibo
1903	Britain completes the conquest of the Sokoto Caliphate
1914	Britain conquers Abeokuta, last independent state in Nigeria
1914	Britain forms the colony and protectorate of Nigeria

0–1969

1960 Oct. 1	Nigeria becomes independent of Britain
1963	Nigeria declares itself a republic
1966	Military takes over the Nigerian government: Lt. Col. Gowon becomes leader of Nigeria
1967 May 30	Eastern Region under Ojukwu declares independence as Biafran civil war breaks out

0–1979

1970 Jan. 12	Biafra surrenders ending the civil war
1975	Gowon is replaced by Gen. Murtala Muhammad
1976 Feb.	Gen. Muhammad is killed in a failed coup attempt: Lt. Gen. Olesegun Obasanjo succeeds as leader
1978 May	Obasanjo approves a democratic constitution
1979 Aug.	Alhaji Shehu Shagari's National Party of Nigeria wins federal elections

0–1989

1983 Dec.	Shagari's government is overthrown by a military coup: Maj. Gen. Muhammad Buhari becomes president
1985 Aug.	Buhari overthrown by Maj. Gen. Ibrahim Babangida

0–1999

1991	Nigerian government is transferred from Lagos to Abuja
1993 Jun.	Social Democratic Party of Moshood Abiola wins federal elections
1993 Aug.	Babangida annuls the election result
1993 Nov.	Government overthrown by military coup of Gen. Sanni Abacha
1994 June	Abiola declares himself president and is arrested for treason
1995 Nov.	Nigeria expelled from the Commonwealth
1998 Jun.	Death of Abacha: he is succeeded by Gen. Abdulsalam Abubakar
1999 Feb.	Olesegun Obasanjo is elected president
1999 May	Military government hands over power to president Obasanjo

00–

2000	Muslim-Christian clashes occur in the north
2001	Obasanjo, President Mbeki of South Africa and President Bouteflika of Algeria launch a New Partnership for African Development, calling on the rest of the world to partner Africa in a new era of economic and political progress
2002	Ethnic conflict continues in Nigeria

British protectorate
This stamp was issued in 1912, two years before northern Nigeria became incorporated into Nigeria.

New republic
In October 1963 Nigeria declared itself a republic, a fact celebrated in this souvenir edition of the *Nigerian Morning Post*.

Soldier
Biafra seceded from Nigeria in 1967. The civil war continued until 1970 when Nigerian troops put down the rebellion.

© DIAGRAM

73

Rwanda

An independent nation
This stamp was issued in 1962 to celebrate Rwanda's newly-acquired status.

Rwanda's first inhabitants were the Twa, who now make up only one percent of the population. During the first millennium, the ancestors o the modern Hutu reached the area. Then, around 600 years ago, the T people arrived. The Tutsi kingdoms dominated the Hutu, treating then slaves. In 1897, Germany made the area called Ruanda-Urundi part of German East Africa. After World War I, the League of Nations asked Belgium to rule the area. In 1959, a Hutu uprising against the Tutsi caused 10,000 deaths and, in 1961, the people of Ruanda (Rwanda) voted to make their country a republic, while Urundi (Burundi) remair a monarchy. Both countries became independent on July 1, 1962.

Grégoire Kayibanda, Rwanda's first president, attempted to unite the country. Kayibanda was reelected in 1965 and 1969, but in 1973, following renewed Hutu-Tutsi conflict, a military coup brought Juvén. Habyarimana to power. He dissolved parliament and became presiden In 1978, Rwanda became a one-party regime. In 1990, a Tutsi rebel force, the Rwandan Patriotic Front (RPF), formed from the refugees ir Uganda, invaded Rwanda. They were defeated with French help. In 1991, Rwanda restored a multiparty system but, in 1994, Habyariman: and Burundi's president were killed when the plane on which they wer traveling was apparently shot down by Hutu extremists. Many Hutu began a campaign of genocide. But the RPF defeated the Hutu and set a government of national unity. But more than 2 million people fled in exile, mainly into Zaire (now the Democratic Republic of Congo). Tut forces in Zaire helped to overthrow Zaire's government in 1997. In 20 Paul Kagame, who had been Rwanda's effective ruler since he ended t genocide in 1994, became president.

Leaders

Habyarimana, Juvénal
(1937–1994)
Major General Juvénal Habyarimana took power following a bloodless coup in 1973, ousting President Kayibanda. He ruled until he was killed, together with President Ntaryamira of Burundi, in a plane crash in 1994. Both men were Hutu. Their deaths provoked Hutu-Tutsi conflict.

Kagame, Paul
(1957–)
A former Vice-President, Major General Paul Kagame became president of Rwanda in 2000. Kagame grew up in Uganda where his parents had fled to escape Hutu violence. He joined Yoweri Museveni in the struggle to overthrow President Obote. In office, Kagame stressed his Rwandan rather than his Tutsi identity.

Kayibanda, Grégoire
(1924–)
Grégoire Kayibanda, a Hutu, became the first president of Rwanda when the country beca independent in 1962. In 1963, a Tutsi force tried to seize power a this provoked the Hutu into viole reprisals. Kayibanda was reelected in 1965 and 1965. But in 1973, a military group led by Habyarimana deposed him.

nda timeline

10th centuries		Hutu farmers migrate to the Rwanda region
15th century		The Tutsis invade Rwanda from the north and conquer the Hutus
century		
	1897 CE	The Germans conquer Ruanda-Urundi (the region of modern Rwanda and Burundi)
–1949	**1916**	Belgian troops occupy Ruanda-Urundi
	1923	The League of Nations mandates Ruanda-Urundi to Belgium
	1946	Ruanda-Urundi becomes a UN trust territory administered by Belgium
–1959	**1959**	Grégoire Kayibanda forms the Party for Hutu Emancipation (PARMEHUTU)
	1959	Hutu-Tutsi violence breaks out after the mysterious death of King Mutara III
–1969	**1960**	The Hutus win control of local legislature in elections
	1961	Ruanda votes to become an independent republic, Urundi to become an independent kingdom (Burundi)
	1962 July 1	Rwanda becomes independent. The Hutu leader Kayibanda, becomes president
	1965	Kayibanda is reelected president
	1969	Kayibanda is elected to a third term as president
–1979	**1973**	Kayibanda is ousted by a military coup: Hutu Maj. Gen. Juvénal Habyarimana becomes president
	1978	Rwanda becomes a one party state
–1989	**1980**	Habyarimana purges the ruling party, PARMEHUTU
	1983	President Habyarimana is reelected unopposed
–1999	**1990**	The Rwandan Patriotic Front (RPF), a Tutsi rebel movement based in Uganda, begins attacks on the government
	1991	A multiparty constitution is introduced after another RPF invasion
	1994 Apr.	Habyarimana and Ntaryamira of Burundi are killed when their plane is shot down by Hutu extremists
	1994 May	Hutu extremists kill 750,000 Tutsi in a campaign of genocide
	1994 Jul.	The RPF defeats Hutu forces and forms a government of national unity under a moderate Hutu president and prime minister: 2 million Hutus flee, most of them to Zaïre (now Dem. Rep. of Congo)
	1995	The government begins holding war crimes trials
	1996	Many Hutus return to Rwanda after attacks on their refugee camps by Zaïrian Tutsi rebels
	1998	After being convicted of genocide, 22 Hutus are executed
–	**2000**	Paul Kagame, a Tutsi, replaces the moderate Hutu President Pasteur Bizimungu
	2001	Rwanda's first ever local elections are held. A new flag and national anthem are introduced to emphasize national unity

Allied kingdoms
This stamp was issued before Ruanda-Urundi became independent nations in 1962.

A casualty of war
The conflict in Rwanda in the 1990s between the Tutsi-dominated rebels and the majority Hutu people produced many tragedies, such as this orphaned child.

Senegal

France began to take control of what is now Senegal in the early 17th century. The area finally became a French colony in 1882. In 1895, Senegal became part of French West Africa, with Dakar as its capital. April 1959, Senegal and Mali united to form the Federation of Mali, which became independent on June 20, 1960. But, Senegal soon left federation and, on August 20, 1960, it declared itself the Republic of Senegal. Its first president was Léopold Sédar Senghor, who had four the socialist Senegalese Progressive Union (UPS) in 1948. In 1962, Mamadou Dia, the prime minister, tried but failed to overthrow Sengl In 1963, Senghor abolished the post of prime minister. In 1966, Seneg became a one-party state. Several attempted coups occurred, while lo droughts seriously damaged the economy in the late 1960s and 1970s Senghor began to return to multiparty democracy in the 1970s. In 197 he restored the post of prime minister and, in 1974, he legalized politi parties. In 1981, Senghor retired, and was was succeeded by Abdou Diouf, the former prime minister.

In 1981, Senegal put down a rebellion against Gambia's governmen In 1982, the two countries set up an organisation which became know as the Confederation of Senegambia. But this confederation was abandoned in 1989. In 1990, Diouf had to handle violence in the nortl where border clashes occurred with Mauritania. He also had to deal w secessionists in the southern province of Casamance. Diouf maintaine good relations with France, which provided both aid and military advisers to Senegal. In 2000, Abdoulaye Wade defeated Diouf in presidential elections. Wade's election ended 40 years of socialist rule and his supporters won a parliamentary majority in 2001.

French railroad
This railroad was built by the French in the 1880s to link the port of Dakar with Senegal. It enabled the colonists to transport goods from inland to the coast with greater efficiency.

Leaders

Diouf, Abdou
(1935–)
Abdou Diouf was prime minister of Senegal from 1970–1981, when he succeeded Léopold Senghor as president. He was elected president in 1983 and reelected in 1988 and 1993, but defeated in 2000. In 1981, he put down a rebellion in Gambia. The confederation set up by the two countries ended in 1989.

Senghor, Léopold Sédar
(1906–2001)
Senghor served as Senegal's president from 1960 until he voluntarily retired in 1981. He worked to modernize his country, combat corruption, and encourage international cooperation. He made Senegal a one-party state in 1966, but later restored democracy. He was also a distinguished poet and philosopher.

Wade, Abdoulaye
(1926–)
After four unsuccessful attempt become elected president of Senegal, Abdoulaye Wade defeated Abdou Diouf in electio in 2000. A lawyer and academi Wade had been in exile and imprisoned several times. He had also served as a minister in Diouf's government. In 2001, his supporters won a majority in elections.

egal timeline

19th century

1240–1400 CE	The empire of Mali dominates the Senegal region
–18th centuries	The Fulani Wolof kingdom dominates much of Senegal
1445	Portuguese navigators explore the coast of Senegal
1617	The Dutch establish a trading post on Gorée island
1626	The French build a trading post at the mouth of the Sénégal River
1677	The French take over Gorée Island from the Dutch
1763	Britain expels the French from Senegal
1765	Britain creates the colony of Senegambia, incorporating parts of Senegal and Gambia
1783	Britain cedes Senegal back to France

century

19th century	Islam becomes the main religion in Senegal
1848	France abolishes slavery in Senegal
1854	France begins to establish control over inland areas
1882	Senegal becomes a French colony
1895	Senegal is incorporated into the French West Africa colony
–1949 **1946**	Senegal becomes an overseas territory of France
1948	Senghor founds the Senegalese Progressive Union
–1959 **1956**	Senegal is granted internal self-government
1959	Senegal and the French Sudan join to form the Federation of Mali
–1969 **1960 Jun. 20**	The federation of Mali becomes independent
1960 Aug. 20	Senegal withdraws from the federation and becomes the Republic of Senegal: Senghor is first president
1962	The prime minister Mamadou Dia attempts unsuccessfully to overthrow president Senghor
1963	Senghor abolishes the office of prime minister
1966	Senegal becomes a one-party state
–1979 **1970**	The office of prime minister is restored by a referendum
1974	Political parties are legalized
–1989 **1981**	President Senghor resigns: the prime minister Abdou Diouf becomes president
1982	Senegal and Gambia form the confederation of Senegambia
1983	Diouf is reelected to the presidency
1989	Gambia withdraws from Senegambia. Fighting breaks out on the border with Mauritania
–1999 **1991**	Renewed fighting on the border with Mauritania
1992	Armed clashes with Casamance separatists in southern Senegal
1993	Diouf is reelected to the presidency for the third time. A ceasefire is agreed with the Casamance separatists
– **2000**	Abdoulaye Wade, in his fifth attempt to win the presidency, defeats Diouf and becomes president of Senegal.
2001	Wade-led coalition wins an overwhelming victory in parliamentary elections

Senegalese soldiers
African soldiers served in the French colonial army in the mid-1850s.

DAKAR-MERS EL-KEBIR

Propaganda
Germany celebrated the defeat of British and Free French forces who had tried to gain control of Senegal from the port of Dakar, which was the capital of Vichy French West Africa.

© DIAGRAM

Sierra Leone

In 1787, a group of freed slaves landed on the coast of what is now S
Leone. Their settlement became Freetown. After 1807, when Britain
abolished slavery, Freetown became a British base. Many freed slave
settled there. Inland areas became a British protectorate (colony) in 1
Sierra Leone became independent on April 27, 1961. Milton Margai,
first prime minister, died in 1964. His brother Albert took over, but a
coup in 1967 deposed him. In 1968, another coup led to the return of
democracy and Siaka Stevens, leader of the All-People's Congress
(APC), became prime minister. In 1971, Sierra Leone became a repul
and, in 1976, the APC became the only legal party. In 1985, Stevens
handed over power to Major-General Joseph Momoh. But, in 1990,
rebels from Liberia invaded intending to remove Momoh. The rebels
by Foday Sankoh, were called the Revolutionary United Front (RUF
The rebels were driven back with support from Guinea and Nigeria. I
the mid-1990s, the RUF held diamond-mining areas. It used money f
diamond sales to buy weapons.

In 1992, Momoh was overthrown by Captain Valentine Strasser, wl
was deposed in 1996. Ahmad Tejan Kabbah was then elected preside
but he was overthrown in 1997. In 1998, following a Nigerian-led
intervention against the military regime, Kabbah returned from exile.
Civil war broke out again in 1999. Following a ceasefire, a governme
was formed with Foday Sankoh, the RUF leader, as vice-president. T
ceasefire collapsed in 2000. British troops intervened and Sankoh wa
arrested. Another ceasefire was signed in 2000. In 2001, UN troops
helped to disarm the rebels and, in 2002, the war was declared over. I
May 2002, Kabbah won victories in national elections.

Refuge
Many freed slaves were settled at Bathurst (now Banjul) once Sierra Leone became a refuge in the late 1700s.

Leaders

Kabbah, Ahmad Tejan
(1932–)
Ahmad Tejan Kabbah was elected prime minister in 1995. He was deposed in 1997 and went into exile, but returned in 1998. He was reelected president in 2002 after peace had ben restored. Kabbah had earlier worked as a civil servant in Sierra Leone. He also spent 21 years working for the UN Development Program.

Margai, Sir Milton Augustus Stiery
(1895–1964)
Milton Margai was chief minister of Sierra Leone from 1954–1958 and prime minister from 1958 until his death in 1964. He was succeeded by his half-brother Albert Margai. He had earlier studied medicine and became a doctor in Sierra Leone. He formed the Sierra Leone People's Party in 1951, winning elections that year.

Stevens, Siaka Probyn
(1905–1988)
Siaka Stevens was active in th independence struggle, but he out with Milton Margai and set the rival All-People's Congress was an opposition leader until APC won elections in 1967. Fr 1971, Stevens served as president when the country became a republic. Stevens retired from office in 1985.

ra Leone timeline

-19th century

1460 CE Portuguese navigators explore the coast of present-day Sierra Leone

1787 Granville Sharp of the Anti-Slavery Society buys land on Cape Sierra Leone for a settlement of freed slaves

1792 The first 400 freed African-American slaves are settled on the site of present-day Freetown

a century

1807 Britain abolishes the slave trade

1808 Britain makes Freetown a crown colony

1815 Britain starts settling slaves at Freetown

1864 The last of over 50,000 freed slaves are settled at Freetown.

1896 Inland areas of Sierra Leone become a British protectorate

0–1949

1924 The first elected representatives join the Sierra Leone legislative council

0–1959

1951 Freetown is united with Sierra Leone and the colony is granted internal self-government

1952 Milton Margai becomes prime minister of Sierra Leone

0–1969

1961 **Apr. 27** Sierra Leone becomes independent with Milton Margai as prime minister

1964 After the death of Margai, political instability sets in

1967 An indecisive general election is followed by a military coup

1968 The military government is overthrown: Siaka Stevens becomes head of government

0–1979

1971 Sierra Leone becomes a republic with Stevens as president

1978 Sierra Leone becomes a one–party state

0–1989

1981 The Sierra Leone Labor Congress calls a general strike against government economic policy

1985 Stevens retires and is succeeded by Maj. Gen. Joseph Momoh

1987 The government declares a state of economic emergency

0–1999

1991 Corporal Foday Sankoh leads an uprising against Momoh

1992 Capt. Valentine Strasser overthrows Momoh and cancels planned elections: Sankoh leads a second uprising

1996 Ahmad Tejan Kabbah of the Sierra Leone People's Party is elected president: he signs a peace deal with Sankoh

1997 Maj. Johnny Paul Koromah ousts Kabbah in a military coup

1998 Troops from Nigeria overthrow Koromah and restore Kabbah to power

1999 A peace agreement is signed and UN troops enforce it

0–

2000 UN forces are attacked by rebels, but another ceasefire is agreed. Foday Sankoh is arrested and charged with war crimes

2001 Elections are postponed because of the security situation. Disarmament of rebels begins

2002 The war is officially declared over and Kabbah wins a landslide victory in national elections

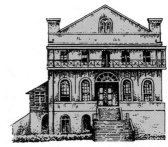

Fourah Bay College
Situated in Freetown, and founded in 1827, this college became a part of the University of Sierra Leone.

Sir Milton Margai
He was the chief minister of Sierra Leone from 1954–1958, and the prime minister from 1958–1964.

© DIAGRAM

Somalia

Aiming to kill
So deeply embedded in the culture of Somalia did killing become, that it was at the heart even of children's games.

Britain began to rule what is now northern Somalia in the 1880s, whi[le] Italy took over the south between 1889 and 1905. Italy invaded Britis[h] Somaliland in 1940, but British forces defeated the Italians in 1941. I[n] 1950, the United Nations asked Italy to prepare Italian Somaliland fo[r] independence. British Somaliland became independent on June 26, 1[960] and, on July 1, 1960, it united with the former Italian Somaliland, creating the Republic of Somalia. The first president, Aden Abdullah Osman, wanted to create a Greater Somalia, linking Somalia with oth[er] Somali-speaking areas in neighboring countries. Abder-Rashid Shermarke, who later became president, rejected Osman's support fo[r] Greater Somalia. Tensions between north and south Somalia mounte[d] 1969, the army, led by Muhammad Siad Barre, staged a coup. Sherm[a] was killed and parliament was abolished.

From 1976, Somalia was a one-party state. Barre obtained foreign a[id] from the Soviet Union, and later from the United States. Armed with weapons from foreign donors, Somalia and Ethiopia waged wars in 1[and again in 1977. In 1991, Mogadishu fell to armed rebels and Barre fled the country. The conflict caused great damage in the south and th[e] Somali National Movement declared the north to be the independent "Somaliland Republic," though it did not receive international recognition. Fighting broke out in the south between armed factions loosely allied to clans. The UN tried unsuccessfully to restore peace between 1992 and 1995. By the early 2000s, the country was divided into the warring south; the northeast, called Puntland; and the norther[n] "Somaliland Republic." In 2000, a peace conference set up an Assem[bly] to operate in Mogadishu, but it applied only to the south.

Leaders

Egal, Mohamed Ibrahim
(1928–2002)
Chosen by the region's parliament, Mohamed Ibrahim Egal served as president of the breakaway and unrecognized "Somaliland Republic" from 1993. He was reelected in 1998. Egal had earlier served as Somalia's prime minister for four days in a transitional government in 1960 and again from 1967 to 1969.

Osman, Aden Abdullah
(1908–)
Aden Abdullah Osman became the first president of Somalia when British and Italian Somaliland were united in 1960. He favored the creation of a Greater Somalia which would include Somalia, Djibouti and the Somali-speaking regions of Ethiopia and Kenya. He was succeeded by Abder-Rashid Shermarke.

Siad Barre, Muhammad
(1919–)
Muhammad Siad Barre becam[e] president of Somalia in Septen[ber] 1969 following a military coup. [His] rule was marked by civil war a[nd] territorial wars with Ethiopia. H[e] was overthrown by rebel forces in 1991. Civil conflict broke out and the country was divided when northerners broke away and set up the "Somaliland Republic."

nalia timeline		
c. 750 CE	The Somalis settle the north of modern Somalia	
11th century	The Somalis convert to Islam	
h century		
1884–1886	Britain establishes a protectorate in northern Somalia	
1889–1905	Southern Somalia becomes an Italian colony	
1897	Italy cedes the Somali Ogaden to Ethiopia	
0–1949	**1912**	The British build border posts to halt Somali infiltration into Kenya
	1936	After Italy conquers Ethiopia, Italian Somaliland is ruled from Addis Ababa
	1940	Italy occupies British Somaliland
	1941	Britain recaptures British Somaliland and occupies Italian Somaliland
0–1959	**1950**	The UN returns Italian Somaliland to Italy for a 10-year period to prepare it for independence
0–1969	**1960 Jun. 26**	British Somaliland becomes independent
	1960 Jul. 1	The two Somali territories unite to form the independent republic of Somalia
	1969	President Shermarke is assassinated during a military coup: Maj. Gen. Mohammad Siad Barre becomes president
0–1979	**1974**	War breaks out between Somalia and Ethiopia over the Ogaden region
	1976	Siad Barre sets up the Somali Revolutionary Socialist Party as the only legal political party
	1977	Somalia occupies the Ogaden
	1978	Ethiopia recovers the Ogaden
	1979	Drought results in food shortages
0–1989	**1988**	Somalia and Ethiopia sign a peace treaty
0–1999	**1991**	The rebel United Somali Congress overthrows the military government and captures Mogadishu. Civil war breaks out between rival clans and in the north the Somali National Movement declares the independent Somaliland Republic
	1993 May	A UN peacekeeping force is sent into Somalia
	1993 Jun.	Mohammad Farah Aidid attacks UN peacekeepers
	1993 Oct.	A bungled attempt to capture Aidid leaves 18 US soldiers and hundreds of Somali civilians dead
	1994 Mar.	US troops are withdrawn from Somalia
	1996	Gen. Aidid is killed fighting a rival faction
	1997	The UN begins a new aid program after southern Somalia is devastated by floods
	1998	Rival clan leaders declare their commitment to peace
0–	**2000**	A conference in Djibouti sets up a three-year transitional National Assembly to operate in Mogadishu
	2001	A drought causes crop failure
	2002	The transitional government arrests 11 people suspected of having links with terrorist groups

Vittorio Emanuele III
A four-*bese* (Somalian currency) coin with the head of the then Italian king, issued in 1909, when the southeastern coast of the Somalia region was under Italian control.

Abder-Rashid Shermarke
A firm advocate of self-determination for Somalians, he was assassinated in a military coup in 1969.

© DIAGRAM

South Africa

A graphic protest
This 1986 poster highlighted the injustices of the apartheid regime.

Sharpeville Massacre
69 people were killed and over 100 injured in this 1960 demonstration.

In 1910, Britain created the Union of South Africa, a self-governing country in the British Empire. In 1912, opposition to white rule was expressed in the formation of the African National Congress (ANC). Two years later, the Afrikaners, who had suffered defeat in the Secon Anglo-Boer War (1899–1902), founded the National Party to protect their interests. In World War I, South Africa occupied Southwest Afr (now Namibia) and, after the war, the League of Nations mandated S Africa to rule the area, which it continued to do until 1990. In 1948, t National Party, which represented the interests of the Afrikaner peopl won power in elections in which the voters were all white. The Natio Party introduced apartheid (the racist doctrine of "separate development"). The ANC, together with other black, Colored, Asian, white liberal groups, strongly opposed the racist laws. In 1961, South Africa, stung by international protests, became a republic. Internation sanctions were imposed on South Africa in the 1980s, damaging the country's economy.

In 1989, the Nationalist President F. W. de Klerk began talks with t ANC which ended with the movement being legalized. The ANC lea Nelson Mandela, imprisoned since 1962, was released. Racist laws w repealed and, in 1994, South Africa held its first nonracial elections. ANC won a majority and Mandela became president. He pursued policies of "reconciliation" aimed at healing South Africa's divided society. In 1999, Mandela retired. He was succeeded by Thabo Mbek who faced many problems, including great poverty in black areas, a h crime rate, and the incidence of HIV and AIDS – in 2000, a UN repo stated that nearly 10 percent of South Africans were infected.

Leaders

de Klerk, Frederik Willem
(1936–)
De Klerk became president of South Africa in 1989. He swiftly dismantled the racist policies of apartheid and set up nonracial elections in 1994. After the elections, de Klerk and Thabo Mbeki became vice-presidents of South Africa. In 1993, de Klerk shared the Nobel Peace Prize with Nelson Mandela.

Mandela, Nelson Rolihlahla
(1918–)
Nelson Mandela served as president of South Africa from 1994 until 1999. He was a leader of the ANC before it was banned in 1960 and he was imprisoned between 1962 and 1990. In office, he sought to reconcile rival ethnic and political groups. After his retirement, he acted as mediator in several African disputes.

Mbeki, Thabo
(1942–)
Thabo Mbeki became deputy president of South Africa in 19 and, in 1999, he succeeded Nelson Mandela as president. 1975, he became the younges member of the ANC executive office, Mbeki was criticized for his view that HIV was not the only cause of the AIDS epidemic and that poverty was a main contributory factor.

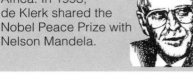

th Africa timeline

1652 CE The Dutch East India Company establishes a supply base at the site of present-day Cape Town

1770 The Boers fight their first war against the Xhosa

1795 Britain occupies the Cape Colony

century

1814 The Netherlands cedes the Cape Colony to Britain

1818–1828 The Zulu conqueror Shaka builds the kingdom of KwaZulu

1836 The Boers begin the Great Trek into the interior to escape British rule

1843 Britain annexes Natal

1852 The Transvaal becomes a Boer republic

1854 The Orange Free State becomes a Boer republic

1867 Diamonds are discovered near Kimberley

1877 Britain annexes the Transvaal

1879 Britain conquers the Zulu kingdom

1880–1881 The First Anglo-Boer War: Transvaal defeats the British

1899 Transvaal and the Orange Free State declare war on Britain beginning the Second Anglo-Boer War (the South African War)

0–1949 **1902** Peace of Vereeniging ends the Anglo-Boer war: the Boer republics become British colonies

1910 The Union of South Africa is formed and becomes an independent dominion within the British Empire

1914 South African forces occupy German Southwest Africa

1920 The League of Nations mandates Southwest Africa to South Africa

1931 Britain grants South Africa full independence

1948 The National Party comes to power under Malan and introduces apartheid

0–1969 **1961** South Africa becomes a republic and leaves the Commonwealth

1962 Nelson Mandela is jailed for sabotage and treason

0–1979 **1976** Over 600 blacks killed by police during the Soweto uprising

0–1989 **1986** Economic sanctions are imposed on South Africa by the Commonwealth, the European Community and the US

1989 F. W. de Klerk becomes prime minister

0–1999 **1990 Feb.** The ANC is legalized and Nelson Mandela is released from prison

1990 Mar. South Africa grants independence to Namibia

1990–1991 The government repeals the apartheid laws

1994 Nelson Mandela is elected president

1999 Nelson Mandela retires as president, Thabo Mbeki of the ANC is elected president

0– **2000** Mbeki faced criticism for his views on the AIDS epidemic and also his pro-business economic policies

2002 The High Court orders the government to give anti-retroviral drugs to HIV-positive pregnant mothers in state hospitals

The Great Trek
Afrikaners migrated inland from the Cape of Good Hope to avoid oppressive British rule from 1836–1848.

Separate amenities
Legislation in 1952 ensured that separate facilities should be provided for different races, even stairways.

Township law
Armed police enforced the law without compromise in the black townships.

© DIAGRAM

83

Sudan

Sudan became fully independent with an elected government on Janu 1, 1956. Since then, successive governments, both civilian and militar have failed to reconcile the interests of the Muslim Arabs in the north and the black Africans in the south, who practise traditional African religions or Christianity. The southerners also object to the use of Ara as the national language and of Islamic law in the courts.

In 1958, General Ibrahim Abboud overthrew the elected governme He abolished political parties and set up a military regime. He used military means in an attempt to solve the problem of reconciling the cultures of the north and south. In 1964, a general strike occurred and civilian rule was restored. But, in 1969, Colonel Gaafar Muhammad Nimeiri seized power. Like Abboud, he abolished political parties, an 1972, he became Sudan's president. In 1973, Sudan became a one-par state. Nimeiri gave the southern provinces regional self-government, l he ended this policy in 1983, when he imposed Islamic law throughou Sudan. This caused a rebellion and the Sudanese People's Liberation Army launched attacks on government-held sites in the south.

In 1985, a group of officers deposed Nimeiri, and multiparty electio were held in 1986. However, in 1989, Brigadier General Omar Hassa Ahmed al-Bashir seized power. He dissolved parliament, and ruled through a military council. Attempts to restore peace in the south faile and the fighting continued, causing great suffering. Elections were he in Sudan in 1996 and 2000. In 1998, the government declared itself willing to hold a referendum on whether the south should be allowed secede. However, no date was suggested. It also became clear that the was no agreed definition of "the south."

Colonel Nimeiri
While president of Sudan (1972–1985), he imposed Islamic law throughout the country.

Leaders

Abboud, Ibrahim
(1901–1983)
Abboud seized power in Sudan in 1958 and set up a military government. He abolished all democratic institutions. But many professional people in Sudan opposed his military policies aimed at overcoming resistance in the south. He was overthrown in 1964 following a general strike against his government.

Bashir, Omar Hassan Ahmad al-
(1944–)
Brigadier-General Omar al-Bashir overthrew Sudan's civilian government led by Sadiq al-Mahdi in June 1989. He served as president of the Revolutionary Command Council for National Salvation. al–Bashir was appointed president of Sudan in 1993 and was subsequetly reelected president in 1996 and 2000.

Garang de Mabior, John
(1946–)
In 1983, John Garang, a memb of the Dinka ethnic group in southern Sudan, became lead the rebel Sudanese People's Liberation Movement and its military wing, the Sudanese People's Liberation Army. He opposes the use of the Arabic language in schools and the imposition of *sharia* (Islamic holy) law.

an timeline

c. 1700 BCE	The kingdom of Kush (Nubia) develops
712 BCE	The Nubians conquer Egypt
671 BCE	The Nubians are driven out of Egypt by the Assyrians.
590 BCE	The center of Nubian power shifts south to the city of Meroë in central Sudan
c. 350 CE	Meroë is conquered by the Ethiopian kingdom of Axum
c. 540	The Nubians are converted to Christianity
1505	Alwa, the last Christian kingdom in present-day Sudan, is conquered by African Funj tribes
n century	Funj kingdom is at the peak of its power
n century	
1821	Egypt conquers the Funj
1869	Khedive Ismail of Egypt sends Samuel Baker on an expedition up the White Nile
1873	Baker establishes Egyptian control on the upper Nile
1874	Ismail appoints the British general Charles George Gordon governor of Sudan
1881	Muhammad Ahmad proclaims himself the Mahdi ("messiah") and leads a revolt against Egypt
1885	The Mahdi captures Khartoum and Gordon is killed
1898	Anglo-Egyptian force defeats the Sudanese at Omdurman
1899	Joint Anglo-Egyptian government of the Sudan established
0–1949 · **1948**	Sudan is granted a legislative council
0–1959 · **1953**	Britain and Egypt grant self-government to Sudan
1956	**Jan. 1** Sudan becomes an independent republic
1958	Gen. Ibrahim Abboud becomes president after a military coup
0–1969 · **1964**	General strike forces the military government to step down
1969	Col. Gaafar Nimeiri seizes power after a military coup
0–1979 · **1971**	Nimeiri becomes president of Sudan
1972	Nimeiri gives the southern provinces an autonomous regional government ending the rebellion
1973	Nimeiri's Sudanese Socialist Union (SSU) becomes the only legal political party
0–1989 · **1983**	Rebellion breaks out in the Christian south after Nimeiri imposes Islamic law throughout the country
1985	Nimeiri ousted by a military coup and the SSU is disbanded
1986	Elections are held for a new legislature
1989	Brig. Gen. Omar Hassan Ahmed al-Bashir overthrows al-Mahdi in an Islamic fundamentalist military coup
0–1999 · **1993**	The military appoint al-Bashir president
1996	Al-Bashir is elected president, taking 75 percent of the vote
0– · **2000**	Al-Bashir is reelected president, with 86 percent of the vote
2001	Government forces launch a major offensive against the Nuba people of central Sudan
2002	Sudan's government and southern rebels sign a peace accord

A royal crown
Made of silver and gold, this ornate crown formerly belonged to a Nubian king.

Flight from the battlefield
Sudanese forces were defeated by an Anglo-Egyptian army at the Battle of Omdurman in 1898.

©DIAGRAM

Swaziland

Britain took control of Swaziland in 1902. It ruled the country until it became independent as a constitutional monarchy on September 6, 19[...] At first, the constitution placed limits on the power of the king, Sobhu[...] II. As a result, in 1973, Sobhuza suspended the constitution and banne[...] all political parties. He then ruled directly, with the assistance of pers[...] advisers and a Swazi National Council appointed by him. Under a ne[...] constitution, the king appointed a legislature in 1979, but he kept the power of veto. Sobhuza died in 1982 and, in 1983, one of his many s[...] Makhosetive, was named heir. He was crowned Mswati III in 1986. Although only 19 years old, he soon revealed his authority. He dissol[...] the Supreme Council of State set up by his father and dismissed the prime minister. In 1992, he suspended the constitution and ruled by decree. But he introduced some reforms. In 1993, he allowed directly elected members to be appointed to the legislature and he also permitt[...] elections by secret ballot instead of by a show of hands. But such changes did not satisfy those who wanted democracy.

In 1995, protesters burned down the parliament building. As tensio[...] mounted, Mswati set up a commission to review the constitution. But this commission was packed with members of the royal family and others who had much to lose should reforms occur. Elections were he[...] in 1998, but the turnout was low. This was partly because political pa[...] were banned. In the early 21st century, Mswati showed little enthusia[...] for sharing power and continued to rule by decree. Freedom of expression was severely restricted and criticism of the king was banne[...] Swaziland also faced many other problems; for example, about a qua[...] of the population were thought to be infected with HIV.

Founder of a nation
Mswati I, who ruled from 1845–1865, gave his name to the Swazi nation, and made his kingdom one of the most powerful in the Southern Africa region.

Leaders

Mswati I
(c. 1820–1865)
Mswati I was the founder of the Swazi nation and king of the Ngwane kingdom. Mswati ruled from 1845 until 1865. He was a great general and made his kingdom one of the most powerful in the region.
During his reign, his kingdom extended as far north as present-day Zimbabwe.

Mswati III
(1968–)
Son of Sobhuza II, Mswati III became king of Swaziland in 1986. He was chosen as heir to the throne following the death of his father in 1982. He was officially made king when he reached the age of 18. Mswati introduced some reforms, but opposition groups favored a more democratic type of government.

Sobhuza II
(1899–1982)
Sobhuza II became king of Swaziland in 1922 and worked [...] make his country prosperous. H[...] became head of state in 1968 a[...] regained land that had been ta[...] by European settlers. In 1973, [...] abolished the existing democratic constitution and ruled by decree. He introduced a new constitution in 1979.

aziland timeline

c. 1770 CE	Chief Ngwane II leads his Dlamini clan into present-day Swaziland

h century

1830s	British traders and Boer farmers visit Swaziland
1836	Ngwane's successor, Mswati (Mswazi) II, names his people "Swazi" after himself
1865	Mswati II allies with the British against the Boers
1878	Influx of Europeans after gold is discovered in Swaziland
1881	Britain guarantees the independence of Swaziland
1884	The Boer republic of Transvaal guarantees the independence of Swaziland
1890	A provisional government of Swazi, British and Boer representatives is formed
1894	Britain agrees that Transvaal should establish a protectorate over Swaziland
1899	The infant Sobhuza II becomes king under a regency

00–1949	**1902**	Following their victory in the Anglo-Boer War, the British take control of Swaziland
	1903	Swaziland is declared a British protectorate
	1921	King Sobhuza II begins personal rule
60–1969	**1964**	The royalist Imbokodvo party wins elections to a newly created legislature
	1968 Sept. 6	Swaziland becomes an independent constitutional monarchy under king Sobhuza II
70–1979	**1973**	King Sobhuza suspends the constitution and assumes direct rule
	1979	King Sobhuza appoints a new legislature but retains the power of veto
80–1989	**1982**	Death of King Sobhuza after a reign of 82 years
	1983	Sobhuza II's son Makhosetive is named heir to the throne
	1984	State university is closed following student protests
	1986	Makhosetive is crowned king, assuming the name Mswati III
90–1999	**1992**	King Mswati suspends the legislature and rules by decree
	1993	For the first time directly elected members of parliament are appointed to the legislature
	1995	Democracy protesters from the Swaziland Youth Congress burn down the parliament building
	1996	A constitutional committee is appointed to consider plans to democratize the country
	1998	King Mswati announces a major environmental restoration program
00–	**2001**	King Mswati III imposes a five-year sex ban on young girls to halt the spread of HIV-AIDS. He is criticized for taking a 17-year-old schoolgirl as his eighth wife
	2002	Poor harvests leave nearly 40 percent of the population on the verge of starvation

A royal visit
King Sobhuza II and some of his supporters visited London in 1925 to assert what they believed to be their superior claim in a dispute over ownership of land in Swaziland.

Ready for action
A stamp, issued in 1968, which depicted a Swazi warrior in full battle dress, armed with both a shield and an *assegai* (spear).

© DIAGRAM

Tanzania

March past
The People's Militia in Tanzania comprised women as well as men.

In 1891, Germany took control of mainland Tanzania and made it a colony called German East Africa. Meanwhile, Britain made Zanziba protectorate (colony) in 1890. During World War I, Britain gained control of German East Africa and renamed it Tanganyika. In 1954, a group of nationalists opposed to British rule formed the Tanganyika African National Union (TANU). Tanganyika became independent or December 9, 1961. TANU's leader, Julius Nyerere, the country's first prime minister, was elected president in 1962, when Tanganyika beca a republic. Zanzibar won its independence on December 10, 1963 and on April 26, 1964, Tanganyika and Zanzibar merged to form the Unit Republic of Tanzania. In 1964, TANU united with Zanzibar's Afro-Shirazi Party to form the *Chama Cha Mapinduzi* (CCM), which becar the sole legal party. Nyerere believed in "African socialism," familyhc and self-reliance. He wanted rural people to move into large villages, with their own schools and health services. Many people moved voluntarily. But in the 1970s, several million people refused to move a they were shifted forcibly into the villages.

Tanzania faced several problems with its neighbors. In 1975, with Chinese aid, a railway was built from Tanzania to Zambia. This helpe Zambia by giving it an outlet to the sea through a friendly country. Th in 1978, Tanzanian troops helped to overthrow the Ugandan dictator I Amin. Nyerere retired in 1985. His successor, President Ali Hassan Mwinyi dropped many of Nyerere's socialist policies, so depriving Zambia of its rail link to the sea. The first multiparty elections, held in 1995, were won by the CCM and Benjamin Mkapa became president. Mkapa was reelected in 2000.

Leaders

Mkapa, Benjamin William
(1938–)
Benjamin Mkapa, leader of the *Chama Cha Mapinduzi* (CCM), became president of Tanzania in 1995 in the first multiparty elections. He was reelected in 2000. In office, he continued the free market policies of his predecessor Ali Hassan Mwinyi. Before entering politics, Mkapa worked as a civil servant and journalist.

Mwinyi, Ali Hassan
(1925–)
Ali Hassan Mwinyi became president of Tanzania in 1985. He was reelected in 1990 and served as president until 1995, when he retired, having completed two terms in office. Mwinyi followed more liberal economic policies than his predecessor. He also introduced a multiparty constitution in 1993.

Nyerere, Julius Kambarage
(1922–1999)
Julius Nyerere led the Tangany African National Union in its struggle against British rule. He became the country's first prim minister in 1961 and its first president in 1962. In 1964, he became president of Tanzania. Nyerere introduced social reforms, but his economic policies were not successful.

‌zania timeline

‌0th century CE		Bantu-speaking peoples settle in Tanzania region
	1698	The sultanate of Oman wins control of Zanzibar
‌h century		
	1858	Richard Burton and John Hanning Speke reach Lake Tanganyika and Lake Victoria
	1867	Britain begins a campaign to destroy Zanzibar's slave trade
	1873	The Sultan of Zanzibar abolishes the slave trade
	1884	German explorer Karl Peters signs treaties with several chiefs in the Tanzania region
	1890	The Sultanate of Zanzibar becomes a British protectorate
	1891	The German East Africa colony is established
‌0–1949	1905	The Maji Maji rebellion against German rule is crushed
1914–1918		The German commander Gen. Paul von Lettow-Vorbeck fights a guerrilla war against allied forces throughout World War I
	1918	British forces occupy the Tanganyika portion of German East Africa
	1920	Tanganyika is mandated to Britain by the League of Nations
	1926	Legislative councils appointed for Tanganyika and Zanzibar
	1946	Tanganyika becomes a UN Trust Territory
‌0–1959	1954	Nyerere forms the Tanganyika African National Union (TANU)
	1958	Tanganyika is granted internal self-government
‌0–1969	1961	**Dec. 9** Tanganyika becomes independent
	1962	Julius Nyerere is elected president
	1963	**Dec. 10** Zanzibar is granted independence
	1964	**Apr. 26** Tanganyika and Zanzibar merge to form the United Republic of Tanzania
	1965	Nyerere merges TANU with Zanzibar's Afro-Shirazi party to form the *Chama Cha Mapinduzi* (CCM) party
	1967	Tanzania, Kenya and Uganda form East African Community
‌0–1979	1975	Tan-Zam (Tanzania-Zambia) railroad is completed
	1977	Internal differences cause the collapse of the East African Community
	1979	Tanzanian troops help overthrow the Ugandan dictator Idi Amin
‌0–1989	1985	Nyerere retires from the presidency: he is succeeded by Ali Hassan Mwinyi
‌0–1999	1992	Opposition parties are legalized
	1994	Around 800,000 refugees from ethnic violence in Rwanda and Burundi flee to Tanzania
	1995	Benjamin Mkapa of the CCM becomes president after the first multiparty elections
	1998	US embassy in Dar es Salaam is destroyed by terrorist blast
	1999	Nyerere dies; Tanzania, Kenya, and Uganda sign a framework agreement establishing a new East African Community, aimed at creating a common market
‌0–	2000	Mkapa is reelected president, with 72 percent of votes cast

Resistance
During the Maji Maji uprising in 1905, Africans fighting against German rule in East Africa, if caught, were punished with severity.

Bomb at US embassy
Tanzania suffered its first major paramilitary attack when a bomb wrecked the US embassy in Dar es Salaam in August 1998.

© DIAGRAM

Togo

In 1884, Germany set up a protectorate on the coast of what is now To
and, in 1899, they established a colony called German Togoland. Duri
World War I, British and French troops invaded German Togoland and
in 1922, the League of Nations mandated Britain to administer the
western third of the colony, with France ruling the rest. In 1956, the
people of British Togoland voted to join Gold Coast and the territory v
incorporated when the Gold Coast became independent as Ghana in
1957. French Togoland became the independent Republic of Togo on
April 27, 1960. Sylvanus Olympio, Togo's president, tried to develop
economy but, in 1963, he was killed by a junior officer, Gnassingbe
Eyadéma, during a military uprising. Olympio was succeeded by Nico
Grunitzky, but, in 1967, Eyadéma (by then a general) seized power.
Eyadéma ruled as a dictator. In 1969, he made the Rally of Togolese
People the only legal party. In the 1970s, Togo's stability made Eyadé
popular. But his harsh methods flouted human rights.

In the early 1980s, the economy began to decline and, in 1985, Frenc
troops helped to put down an attempted coup. In 1991, political partie
were legalized. Eyadéma was elected president in 1993 amid allegatio
of electoral fraud. He was reelected president in 1998, though more
accusations of irregularities clouded the outcome. In 2000, a UN repor
alleged that Burkina Faso's president Blaise Compaoré and Eyadéma
helped the rebel UNITA group in Angola to obtain arms and fuel in
exchange for diamonds mined in the areas occupied by UNITA forces.
Both Burkina Faso and Togo denied the charges. In 2001, an
international commission of inquiry concluded that violations of huma
rights had been committed during the 1998 elections.

Torch and flags
This stamp was issued
in 1960, when French
Togoland became the
independent Republic
of Togo.

Leaders

Eyadéma, Gnassingbe
(1937–)
Before Togo became independent,
Gnassingbe Eyadéma had served
in the French Army. He became
head of state in 1967 following a
coup. In 1969, he set up the Rally
of the Togolese People,
which became Togo's
sole political party.
Under a multiparty
system, he was
reelected president in
1993 and 1998.

Grunitzky, Nicolas
(1937–1994)
Nicolas Grunitzky served as prime
minister of Togo between 1956
and 1958. He became president of
the country in 1963, following the
overthrow of Sylvanus Olympio. He
was a moderate leader, who
maintained close ties with France.
He was deposed and exiled in
1967, following a coup led by
Gnassingbe Eyadéma.

Olympio, Sylvanus
(1902–1963)
Sylvanus Olympio served as
Togo's prime minister from 1958
until 1960, when he became the
country's first president. He tried
develop the economy, especiall
by encouraging foreign investme
and expanding the
phosphate industry.
However, he was
killed in 1963 in a
military coup and
replaced by Nicolas
Grunitzky.

Togo timeline

20th century

1884 CE	Germany sets up a protectorate on the coast	
1899	The German Togoland colony is created	

1900–1949

1914	British and French troops occupy German Togoland
1922	The League of Nations mandates the western third of German Togoland to Britain; the eastern two-thirds are mandated to France
1946	British and French Togolands become UN trust territories

1950–1959

1956	British Togoland votes to join Gold Coast (now Ghana)

1960–1969

1960	**Apr. 27** French Togoland becomes the independent republic of Togo: Sylvanus Olympio becomes the first president
1963	Olympio is assassinated by rebel army officers who make Nicolas Grunitzky president
1967	Grunitzky is overthrown by a military coup led by Gnassingbe Eyadéma
1969	Eyadéma creates the Rally of Togolese People (RPT) and makes it Togo's only legal party

1900–1999

1993	Eyadéma is reelected under a new multiparty constitution
1994	The RPT forms a coalition government with opposition parties
1998	Eyadéma is reelected president

2000–

2000	The UN and the OAU (Organization of African Unity) set up a joint investigation into allegations that Eyadéma and President Compaoré helped the UNITA guerrilla force in Angola obtain weapons in return for diamonds
2001	An international commission reports that systematic violations of human rights occurred during the 1998 elections

An *askari*
Many Africans fought in colonial armies in World War I. Those in uniform were often called *askari*, especially in East Africa.

A former British colony (far left)
In 1956 British Togoland voted to join the Gold Coast (now known as Ghana).

A former French possession (left)
After 1945, Dahomey became an overseas province of France.

© DIAGRAM

91

Tunisia

Tunisia became independent from France on March 20, 1956. In July 1957, the *bey* (Tunisia's local ruler) was deposed and the country beca a republic. Habib Bourguiba, the country's leading nationalist and prir minister, became president. His ruling Neo-Destour party, which was renamed the Destourian Socialist Party in 1964 and the Democratic Constitutional Rally in 1988, introduced such reforms as rights for women and compulsory, free education. Some Islamic fundamentalist were concerned that such reforms would damage Tunisia's Arab-Musl culture. Bourguiba decided that he had to keep his critics under contro and he adopted an increasingly dictatorial manner. In 1975, parliamen made him "president for life."

In 1987, the prime minister General Zine al Abidine Ben Ali remove the elderly and ailing Bourguiba from office and Ben Ali became president. He was fortunate to inherit a stable economy, with a fast-growing tourist industry. In 1988, the government abolished the office "president for life" and ordered the release of all political prisoners. Be Ali also increased press freedoms. However, like Bourguiba, he considered that the Islamic fundamentalists threatened national unity. I 1992, the government accused the Islamic Nahda party of plotting against it. The party was banned. Also, in 1994 Ben Ali prevented fundamentalist parties from participating in the national elections. Ben Ali was reelected president in multi-party elections in 1999. While his party dominated parliament, 20 percent of the seats were reserved for opposition parties. Under Ben Ali, Tunisia experienced violence. Man fundamentalists were arrested and many human rights were suspended but the conflict never reached the scale of the civil war in Algeria.

Comrades in arms
This French stamp, issued in 1943, celebrates the bond between Allied soldiers who liberated Tunisia.

Leaders

Ben Ali, Zine al Abidine
(1936–)
In 1987, Ben Ali removed the ailing Habib Bourguiba from office and became president of Tunisia. He was reelected president in 1989, 1994 and 1999. In 2002, a constitutional change enabled him to stand again in 2004. Ben Ali's rule was marked by economic reforms but criticized for its abuses of human rights.

Bourguiba, Habib ibn Ali
(1903–2000)
The son of an army officer, Bourguiba became secretary of the nationalist Neo-Destour Party in 1934. He soon became the main nationalist leader, calling for an end to French colonial rule. In 1938, all the leaders of the Neo-Destour Party were arrested and Bourguiba was imprisoned in France until 1942. He was again arrested and

detained in 1952 when violence broke out. In 1954, France bega to negotiate with Bourguiba and finally agreed to independence Tunisia.

He became Tunisia's first prin minister in 1956 and the country first president in 1957, when Tunisia became a republic. He was declared president for life i 1975, but was removed from off by a bloodless coup in 1987, as result of his poor state of health.

isian timeline

814 BCE	Phoenicians found the city of Carthage near present-day Tunis
146 BCE	Carthage is conquered by the Roman Empire
439 CE	The Vandals, a Germanic tribe, capture Carthage
534	Carthage is recaptured by the Eastern Roman Empire (Byzantine Empire)
670	The Islamic Arabs invade Tunisia and found Kairouan
800–909	Tunisia becomes independent under the Arab Aghlabid dynasty
909	The Aghlabids are replaced by the Arab Fatimid dynasty
969	The native Berber Zirid dynasty replaces the Fatimids
1236–1574	The Hafsid dynasty rules Tunisia
1535	The Spanish capture Tunis
1573–1574	The Spanish again occupy Tunis
1574	The Ottoman Turks conquer Tunisia
1705	The *beys* (regents) of Tunis become effectively autonomous within the Ottoman empire

h century

1878	Tunisia is recognized as a French sphere of influence at the Congress of Berlin
1881	Tunisia becomes a French protectorate

0–1949	**1920**	The Destour party calls for a national assembly
	1934	Habib Bourguiba founds the Neo-Destour (New Constitution) party
	1942	German and Italian troops occupy Tunisia
	1943	British, US and Free French troops drive the Germans and Italians out of Tunisia
50–1959	**1955**	France grants Tunisia internal self-government
	1956	**Mar. 20** Tunisia becomes independent under the *bey* of Tunis
	1957	Tunisia becomes a republic when the bey abdicates, Bourguiba is elected the first president of Tunisia
60–1969	**1963**	Bourguiba's Democratic Socialist Rally (formerly the Neo-Destour Party) becomes the only legal party
	1964	Land owned by Europeans is nationalized
70–1979	**1975**	Bourguiba becomes president for life
30–1989	**1987**	Prime minister Zine el Abidine Ben Ali removes Bourguiba from office and becomes president in his place
	1988	Opposition parties are legalized
	1989	Tunisia joins Algeria, Libya and Morocco in the Arab Maghrib Union
90–1999	**1992**	The Islamic fundamentalist Nahda party is banned
	1994	Islamic fundamentalist political parties are banned from participating in the first multiparty elections.
	1999	Ben Ali is reelected to the presidency
00–	**2002**	Constitutional changes remove limits of the number of terms president may stand for election

Carthaginian coin
Carthage was originally a Phoenician colony on the coast near Tunis.

Muhammad es Sadek
He was the *bey*, or regent, of Tunis in the mid-19th century.

Hoisting the tricolor
Tunisia became a French protectorate in 1881.

© DIAGRAM

Uganda

Mutesa II
He was the last king of the Bugandan dynasty, and also the first president of the Republic of Uganda.

Buganda, a kingdom to the north and west of Lake Victoria, became a British protectorate (colony) in 1894 and, in 1896, the British extended their territory. Uganda became independent on October 9, 1962. Its first prime minister was Apollo Milton Obote. In 1963, the king of Buganda, Mutesa II, was elected president of Uganda, but Obote dismissed him in 1966. Obote became president in 1967 and he abolished the traditional kingdoms. (The kingdoms were restored in 1992, though their powers were limited.) In 1971, Major General Idi Amin Dada seized power and became president. In 1972, he ordered around 50,000 Asians to leave the country and launched a reign of terror. In 1979, Ugandan rebels led by Yoweri Museveni and aided by Tanzanian troops, deposed Amin, who fled into exile. In 1980, Obote was reelected president. But, following charges of electoral fraud, the National Resistance Movement (NRM) led by Yoweri Museveni, launched a civil war. Obote was removed by a coup in 1985. In 1986, the NRM seized power and Museveni became president. Museveni was opposed to multiparty systems. In 1995, he introduced a nonparty system which he believed was the best way to achieve stability. In 1996 and 2001, Museveni was reelected president.

In the 1990s, insurgent groups, such as the Lord's Resistance Army the north, conducted guerrilla campaigns while, in 1998, Uganda became involved in the civil war in the Democratic Republic of Congo. But the revival of the East African Community with Kenya and Tanzania in the late 1990s held out hope for development. In the 1990s, Uganda was affected by the spread of HIV. But the country's educational campaign brought down the rate of infection dramatically.

Leaders

Amin Dada, Idi
(1925–)
Idi Amin Dada became army commander in 1968. He seized power in 1971 and became president. His regime was harsh and brutal. He expelled Uganda's Asian population and murdered thousands of his opponents. He was deposed in 1979 and fled into exile, finally settling in Saudi Arabia.

Museveni, Yoweri Kaguta
(1945–)
Yoweri Museveni took part in the overthrow of Idi Amin Dada in 1979. He became president in 1986, after his guerrilla forces had seized power. His critics opposed his policy of nonparty government, but he claimed that political parties encouraged ethnic divisions. He was reelected president in 1996 and 2001.

Obote, Apollo Milton
(1924–)
Milton Obote led Uganda to independence in 1962 and served as its first prime minister. In 1966 he dismissed the president, King Mutesa II of Buganda, and made himself executive president. Obote was deposed in 1971 by Idi Amin Dada. He again became president in 1980 and was deposed in 1985.

anda timeline

1862 CE	John Hanning Speke reaches Buganda during his search for the source of the Nile
1894	Buganda becomes a British protectorate
1896	The British protectorate is extended to Bunyoro, Toro, Ankole, and Busoga

)0–1949

1900	Buganda's chiefs sign a treaty accepting British protection
1904	Cotton is introduced and becomes a major cash crop
1921	A colonial legislative council is set up
1931	Railroad between Kampala and Mombasa is completed
1945	The first Africans are appointed to the legislative council

i0–1959

1953	*Kabaka* (King) Mutesa II of Buganda is exiled to Britain for refusing to support British constitutional plans
1955	Mutesa is allowed to return to Uganda after Britain shelves its constitutional plans

i0–1969

1962	**Oct 9** Uganda becomes independent: Apollo Milton Obote becomes prime minister
1963	Mutesa II is elected president
1966	Obote dismisses Mutesa and makes himself president
1967	Uganda becomes a republic and the traditional kingdoms are abolished. Uganda, Kenya and Tanzania form the East African Community

70–1979

1971	Obote is overthrown. Idi Amin Dada becomes president
1972	Amin expels 50,000 Asians and confiscates their assets
1978	Uganda invades Tanzania following a border dispute
1979	Ugandan rebels, aided by Tanzanian troops, overthrow Amin's government

i0–1989

1980	Obote returns from exile and is reelected to the presidency
1981	Yoweri Museveni founds the National Resistance Movement (NRM) and starts a guerrilla war against Obote
1985	Obote is overthrown by another military coup
1986	The NRM captures Kampala and overthrows the military government: Museveni becomes president
1986–1994	National Resistance Council serves as Uganda's legislature

i0–1999

1993	Uganda's four traditional kingdoms are restored
1994	A Constituent Assembly replaces the NRC
1995	A new constitution is approved extending nonparty government for five years
1995–1996	Terrorist campaign in northern Uganda by the Lord's Resistance Army
1996	Museveni is elected president in nonparty elections
1998	Uganda supports rebel forces in the civil war in the Congo
1999	Uganda, Kenya, and Tanzania sign a framework agreement to establish a new African Community, aimed at creating a common market. Uganda and Sudan sign a peace agreement

)0–

2000	An outbreak of the deadly Ebola virus occurs in the north
2001	Museveni is reelected president with 69 percent of the vote

John Hanning Speke
He reached Buganda in 1862, and is believed to be the first European to have visited Lake Victoria, the assumed source of the River Nile.

Mutesa I
He became king of Buganda in 1856 before the country became a British protectorate.

© DIAGRAM

95

Zambia

Inauguration
This stamp, issued in 1967, reflected pride in Zambia's National Assembly Building.

Kariba Dam
Built in the 1950s, the dam necessitated the relocation of thousands of Zambian residents.

In 1924, Britain took over the administration of Northern Rhodesia (now Zambia) from the British South Africa Company. After World War II (1939–1945), many white people in Northern Rhodesia wanted to unite with Southern Rhodesia (now Zimbabwe). In 1953, against much African opposition, Britain set up the Central African Federation of Northern Rhodesia, Southern Rhodesia, and Nyasaland (now Malawi). The federation was dissolved in 1963 and, in 1964, Kenneth Kaunda, leader of the United National Independence Party (UNIP), who had been imprisoned for his activities in opposing the Federation, formed a government. Finally. the country became independent as the Republic Zambia on October 24, 1964, with Kaunda as president.

The new nation faced many problems. Its economy was based on copper mining but, when copper prices fell, the economy came close to collapse. Further, foreign investors were put off by Kaunda's socialist policies. Zambia also faced problems with its southern neighbor Rhodesia (as Southern Rhodesia was then known), especially after 196 when Rhodesia illegally declared itself independent from Britain. However, after 1980, when white minority rule ended in Rhodesia, relations between the countries improved. In 1972, Zambia became a one-party state, with UNIP as the sole legal party. The economic situation worsened in the late 1980s and, in 1990, Kaunda, under great pressure, legalized opposition parties. In elections in 1991, Frederick Chiluba, leader of the Movement for Multiparty Democracy (MMD) defeated Kaunda and became president. He was reelected in 1996 but most people opposed the idea of him serving a third term. In his place, the MMD candidate, Levy Mwanawasa, was elected president in 2001

Leaders

Chiluba, Frederick
(1943–)
Frederick Chiluba became Zambia's second president in 1991, when he defeated Kenneth Kaunda in multiparty elections. He was reelected in 1996, but he stood down in 2001, when his party, the Movement for Multiparty Democracy (MMD), put forward Levy Mwanawasa as their official candidate.

Kaunda, Kenneth David
(1924–)
The first president of Zambia, Kaunda was born in Nyasaland (now Malawi). He opposed the Central African Federation and served time in prison. As president of Zambia from 1964 until 1991, he supported many black nationalist groups in formerly white-minority ruled countries in southern Africa.

Nkumbula, Harry Mwaanga
(1916–1983)
Harry Nkumbula was one of the founders of Zambian nationalism In the early 1950s, he became president of the African National Congress (ANC), the country's fi anticolonial party. He lost suppo in the late 1950s, especially whe Kenneth Kaunda left the ANC in 1958. After independence, he became a major opposition spokesman.

▌mbia timeline

▌-19th century

    c.1000 CE Bantu-speaking peoples settle in the area of modern Zambia

▌h century

1835	Zambia is settled by Nguni people fleeing from Zulu expansion in southern Africa
1855	David Livingstone discovers the Victoria Falls
1889	Cecil Rhodes' British South Africa Company (BSAC) is given responsibility for Barotseland (the area of present-day southern Zambia) by British government charter
1898	The Ngoni rebel against the BSAC

▌0–1949

1900	The BSAC acquires mineral and trading rights from king Lewanika in the area of northern Zambia
1902	Vast copper deposits are discovered at Broken Hill
1911	Barotseland and other BASC territories are united to form the territory of Northern Rhodesia
1924	The British government takes over the administration of Northern Rhodesia
1940	A general strike by African copper miners achieves major improvements in pay and conditions

▌0–1959

1953	Britain forms the Central African Federation of Northern Rhodesia, Southern Rhodesia (now Zimbabwe) and Nyasaland (now Malawi)
1959	Kenneth Kaunda is jailed for nationalist activities

▌0–1969

1960	Kaunda becomes leader of the United National Independence Party (UNIP)
1961	UNIP is outlawed
1963	Britain dissolves the Central African Federation
1964	**Oct. 24** Northern Rhodesia becomes independent as Zambia: Kenneth Kaunda becomes president

▌0–1979

1970	The Zambian government acquires a controlling interest in the copper mining industry
1972	UNIP becomes the only legal party
1973	The white government of Rhodesia (Zimbabwe) closes its border with Zambia
1975	A railroad from the Copperbelt to the Indian Ocean at Dar es Salaam (Tanzania) is built with Chinese help

▌0–1989

1986	Rioting after austerity measures introduced

▌0–1999

1990	Opposition parties are legalized
1991	Frederick Chiluba of the Movement for Multiparty Democracy (MMD) defeats Kaunda in the first multiparty elections
1993	A state of emergency is declared to undermine a campaign of civil disobedience by supporters of UNIP
1996	Chiluba is reelected president
1997	Kaunda is barred from standing for election after failed coup

▌0–

2001	The MMD candidate Levy Mwanawasa is elected president
2002	Many Zambians suffer famine, but the government rejects US aid donations of genetically-modified corn and soya

Under foreign control
This stamp was issued in 1938 when the country was still under the administrative control of the British government.

Copper mine
This is situated in what is known as the "Copperbelt" of Zambia, which has been one of the world's largest producers of copper since the 1930s.

© DIAGRAM

Zimbabwe

An emerging nation
This is a medal struck to celebrate Zimbabwe's independence in 1980.

Military force
Campaigns marked by oppression have ensured Mugabe's frequent reelections.

In 1923, an area called Southern Rhodesia (now Zimbabwe) became a self-governing British colony. In 1953, Britain linked Southern Rhode: Northern Rhodesia, and Nyasaland to form the Central African Federation. But African opposition forced Britain to dissolve it in 196: In 1964, after Northern Rhodesia and Nyasaland had become independent as Zambia and Malawi, Southern Rhodesia became know simply as Rhodesia. When talks with Britain about Rhodesia's future broke down, the prime minister, Ian Smith, declared Rhodesia independent on November 11, 1965. Britain declared his action illegal 1966, a guerrilla war began. The two main opposition groups were the Zimbabwe African People's Union (ZAPU), led by Joshua Nkomo, an the Zimbabwe African National Union (ZANU), which was led, from 1976, by Robert Mugabe. In 1976, ZAPU and ZANU united to form th Patriotic Front (PF). In 1980, Smith agreed to elections, ZANU-PF wo and Mugabe became prime minister and head of the government. Rhodesia became independent as the Republic of Zimbabwe on November 11, 1980.

In 1985, the office of prime minister was abolished and Robert Muga became the executive president. ZANU and ZAPU merged in 1988. Following independence, the white farmers faced problems. From 199 the government began to purchase European-owned land and redistributed the farms to landless Africans. From 2000, the governmer supported a policy of taking over European farms without paying compensation. This policy led to the occupation of white-owned farms violence and the murder of some European farmers. This policy was widely criticized, but, in 2002, Mugabe was reelected president.

Leaders

Mugabe, Robert Gabriel
(1924–)
Mugabe helped to found the Zimbabwe African National Union (ZANU) in 1963. From 1976, ZANU, together with the Zimbabwe African People's Union, waged war against the white minority government. He became prime minister in 1980 and executive president in 1987. He was reelected in 1990, 1996 and 2002.

Nkomo, Joshua Mqabuko Nyongolo
(1917–1999)
Nkomo led the struggle against the Central African Federation in the 1950s and his Zimbabwe African People's Union fought in the guerrilla war in the 1970s. He served under Mugabe between 1980 and 1982. In 1988, Nkomo became one of Zimbabwe's two vice-presidents.

Smith, Ian Douglas
(1919–)
Ian Smith became prime ministe of the white-dominated Rhodesia (now Zimbabwe) in 1964. In 196: he illegally declaredindependenc from Britain. Civil war occurred between government troops and guerrillas led by Robert Mugabe and Joshua Nkomo. Smith stepped down in 1979, when a nonracial government was established.

babwe timeline

c.1100 CE	The Karanga people found a state centered on the city of Great Zimbabwe
c.1450	Great Zimbabwe is abandoned

h century

1888	Cecil Rhodes' British South Africa Company (BSAC) obtains extensive mineral rights from the Ndebele king Lobengula
1895	The BSAC territory is named Rhodesia after Cecil Rhodes
1897	Rhodesia is divided into, Southern Rhodesia (now Zimbabwe) and Northern Rhodesia (now Zambia)

0–1949

1922	In a referendum, the white settlers vote to become a self-governing colony rather than join South Africa
1923	Southern Rhodesia becomes a self-governing British colony
1930	The Land Apportionment Act divides the land between whites and Africans, much in favor of the whites

0–1959

1953	Britain forms the Central African Federation from Southern Rhodesia, Northern Rhodesia, and Nyasaland (now Malawi)

0–1969

1960	Africans form the National Democratic Party (NDP)
1962	The white supremacist Rhodesian Front (RF) wins control of the legislature in whites-only elections
1963	The Central African Federation is dissolved
1963	The NDP splits into Zimbabwe African Peoples' Union (ZAPU) under Joshua Nkomo, and the Zimbabwe African National Union (ZANU) under Ndabaningi Sithole
1964	Ian Smith becomes leader of the RF
1965	**Nov. 11** Smith issues a unilateral declaration of independence (UDI), proclaiming "Rhodesia" independent
1966	The battle of Chinhoyi begins a guerrilla war by Africans

0–1979

1976	Nkomo and Robert Mugabe, the new leader of ZANU, unite to form the Patriotic Front (PF)
1979	Rhodesia reverts to colonial status

0–1989

1980	**Feb.** ZANU-PF win British supervised elections: Mugabe becomes prime minister
1980	**Apr. 18** Rhodesia becomes independent as the republic of Zimbabwe
1982	Mugabe dismisses Nkomo from the government
1987	Mugabe becomes president
1988	ZANU and ZAPU merge; Zimbabwe becomes a one-party state

0–1999

1991	Opposition parties are legalized but under conditions which prevent them campaigning effectively
1992	The Land Acquisition Act provides for government purchase of white-owned lands for redistribution to poor Africans

0–

2000	Electors reject proposals for Mugabe to change the constitution
2001	Armed squatters invade white farms
2002	Mugabe is reelected president amid accusations of electoral irregularities. Evictions of white farmers continue

Shona technology
Situated inside the Great Zimbabwe complex, this conical tower is one of the greatest achievements of the Shona civilization.

Cecil Rhodes
He gave his name to the Rhodesian colonies, and tried to impose British rule throughout Southern Africa.

Sisters in arms
Supporters of Ian Smith learn how to shoot to maintain the white supremacist regime in power in 1965.

© DIAGRAM

Cape Verde

Portuguese navigators discovered what is now Cape Verde in the 15th century. The islands became important as an assembly point for African slaves. In the 19th century, the abolition of the slave trade, together with long droughts, ended the islands' prosperity. At first, Portugal governed the Cape Verde islands together with Portuguese Guinea (now Guinea-Bissau) but, in 1879, they became separate Portuguese colonies. In 195 Cape Verde became an overseas province of Portugal and, in 1961, all Cape Verdeans were granted Portuguese citizenship. From the 1950s, th African Party for the Independence of Guinea and Cape Verde (PAIGC fought against Portuguese rule. Cape Verde became independent on Jul 5, 1975. Its first president was Aristides Pereira, who wanted to create a federation between Cape Verde and Guinea-Bissau, which had become independent in 1974. Many problems arose and, in 1980, a coup in Guinea-Bissau ended prospects of federation. The Cape Verde branch o the PAIGC was dissolved. In 1981, the African Party for the Independence of Cape Verde (PAICV) was formed.

The PAICV was the only political party until 1990, when a multipart system was introduced. In January 1991, the PAICV was defeated in elections by the Movement for Democracy (MPD). In February 1991, MPD candidate, Dr António Mascarenhas Monteiro was elected president. In the 1990s, the government began to liberalize the econom by privatizing many industries. The government also encouraged long-term soil and water conservation measures. But Cape Verde remained dependent on overseas aid. In 2001, the ten-year rule of the MPD was ended when the PAICV won a majority in the National Assembly. Its presidential candidate, Pedro Pires, was elected by a narrow majority.

Dr. António Monteiro
A leader of the Movement for Democracy (MPD), he was elected president in Ferbruary, 1991.

Pedro Pires
A member of PAICV, he was elected president of Cape Verde by a narrow majority in 2001.

Cape Verde timeline		
Pre-19th century		
	1455 CE	Cape Verde islands discovered by Portuguese navigators
	1492	Portuguese planters and their African slaves settle the Cape Verde Islands
1950–1959	1956	Pro-independence nationalists set up the *Partido Africano a la Independência do Guiné e Cabo Verde* (PAIGC)
1960–1969	1961	Guerrilla warfare breaks out
1970–1979	1975	Cape Verde Islands become independent of Portugal
1980–1989	1980	Plans for a union with Guinea-Bissau are dropped
	1981	PAIGC changes its name to *Partido Africano de la Independência da Cabo Verde* (PAICV)
1990–1999	1991	Pereira and the PAICV lose power in Cape Verde's first multiparty elections
2000–	2001	The PAICV regains power and Pires becomes president

moros

he northern end of the Mozambique Channel, the islands of Grande
nore (or Njazidja), Anjouan (or Nzwani), and Mohéli together form
Federal Islamic Republic of the Comoros. The fourth and
ernmost island, Mayotte (or Mahoré) is a French dependency.
wever, in 1974, the people on the three western islands voted for
ependence, while a majority of the people of Mayotte voted to stay
er French rule. Independence for the western islands was achieved on
6, 1975 while, in December 1976, Mayotte became a "territorial
ectivity" (an intermediate state between an overseas territory and an
rseas department of France). Because of ethnic and political rivalries,
Comoros have suffered much instability since 1975. In 1975,
sident Abderrahman Ahmed Abdallah was deposed in a coup by Ali
ih, who was backed by French mercenaries. Soilih was overthrown
978 and Abdallah again became president. He made the country an
mic republic and held elections. More attempted coups occurred, one
hich, in 1989, led to the death of Abdallah. The country returned to
ocracy in March 1990 when elections were held.
1997, Anjouan and Mohéli announced their secession from the
noros, stating that they wished to reestablish contact with France. In
tember, about 300 troops from Grande Comore attempted to conquer
ouan. There were further attempts to reunify the islands, including a
oosal to grant greater autonomy to Anjouan and Mohéli, together
a rotating presidency between the islands. Anjouan did not sign the
ement and opposition to the government's proposal to increase the
vers of the two smaller islands mounted on Grande Comore. Political
uption continued to mar the country's development.

President Abdallah
He was the first leader
of an independent
Comoros in 1975.

An independent state
In 1998 some Anjouan
residents lobbied for
independence from
France colonial rule.

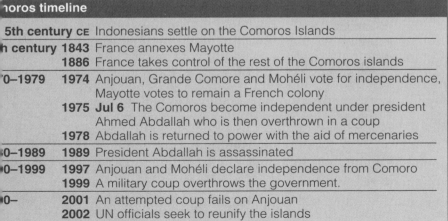

noros timeline

5th century CE	Indonesians settle on the Comoros Islands	
h century	**1843**	France annexes Mayotte
	1886	France takes control of the rest of the Comoros islands
0–1979	**1974**	Anjouan, Grande Comore and Mohéli vote for independence, Mayotte votes to remain a French colony
	1975 Jul 6	The Comoros become independent under president Ahmed Abdallah who is then overthrown in a coup
	1978	Abdallah is returned to power with the aid of mercenaries
0–1989	**1989**	President Abdallah is assassinated
0–1999	**1997**	Anjouan and Mohéli declare independence from Comoro
	1999	A military coup overthrows the government.
0–	**2001**	An attempted coup fails on Anjouan
	2002	UN officials seek to reunify the islands

Bob Denard
A mercenary soldier, he
led *coups d'état* in
Comoros in both 1978
and 1989.

© DIAGRAM

Madagascar

Wildcat
This is the symbol for the Social Democratic Party, led by Philibert Tsiranana, as it appeared on an election poster.

From the late 19th century, France ruled Madagascar. In 1946, the isla became a French overseas territory and it finally became independent the Malagasy Republic on June 26, 1960. The first president, Philiber Tsiranana followed pro-Western policies. He was reelected in 1965 an again in 1972, but allegations of vote-rigging led him to resign. A military group, led by Major-General Gabriel Ramanantsoa, took ove Ramanantsoa distanced his government from France. He ended relatio with South Africa and established contacts with Communist countries 1975, Ramanantsoa handed over power to Colonel Richard Ratsimandrava, who, six days later, was assassinated.

Admiral Didier Ratsiraka, who then became president, renamed the country the Democratic Republic of Madagascar. Relations with Fran improved, but the country kept close links with the Communist world and pursued socialist policies. Elections in 1977 were won by a party formed by Ratsiraka, the National Front for the Defense of the Revolution, which became the country's sole legal political party. Ratsiraka was reelected in 1982. From 1983, the government adopted more free-market policies. Ratsiraka was reelected in 1989 and, in 199 the government permitted the formation of political parties. In 1991, Ratsiraka formed a new government, which adopted a multiparty syst in 1992. In 1993, Albert Zafy was elected president, but he resigned in 1996. In the elections that followed, he was defeated by Ratsiraka. Further presidential elections held in 2002 resulted in stalemate when both candidates, Ratsiraka and Marc Ravalomanana, claimed victory. Ravalomanana eventually became president when Ratsiraka accepted electoral defeat, and subsequently left the country.

Leaders

Ramanantsoa, Gabriel
(1906–1979)
Ramanantsoa became president of Madagascar in 1972, following the resignation of Philibert Tsiranana in the face of strikes and riots. He was popular at first when he maintained order. He prosecuted corrupt officials and released political prisoners. But, following an attempted coup, he handed power over to the military.

Ratsiraka, Didier
(1936–)
A former naval officer, Ratsiraka became head of state in 1975. He was a staunch nationalist and reformer. Despite several attempted coups, he served as president from 1973–1975. He returned to office in 1996, but further election results in 2002 were disputed as both candidates claimed victory.

Tsiranana, Philibert
(1912–)
Tsiranana became Madagasca first president in 1959. He was reelected in 1965 and 1972, an accusations of vote-rigging. In office, his pro-South African policies were widely criticized. In 1972 poor health and demonstrations led him to resign and hand over power to Major-General Gabriel Ramanantsoa.

Madagascar timeline

–5th centuries	Madagascar is settled by peoples from Indonesia
–13th centuries	Muslims from East Africa settle the north of the island
1500 CE	The Portuguese navigator Diogo Dias becomes the first European to visit Madagascar
17th century	Foundation of the kingdom of Merina
1680–1720	Madagascar is a important base for pirates
1787–1810	Merina wins control of most of Madagascar under King Nampoina

century

1817	Britain recognizes King Radama as king of all Madagascar
1845	Queen Ranavalona I defeats a British and French invasion and expels European missionaries and traders
1861	Death of Queen Ranavalona: King Radama II gives concessions to a French trading company
1883–1885	The first Franco-Merina war: Merina cedes the northern town of Diego Suarez to France
1890	France declares Madagascar a protectorate
1895	The second Franco-Merina War: France occupies the capital Antananarivo after Merina refuses to submit to French rule
1896	Madagascar is declared a French colony
1897	France deposes Queen Ranavalona III, the last monarch of Madagascar

0–1949	**1920**	A moderate nationalist movement calling for citizenship rights for the Malagasy is suppressed by France
	1947	A pro-independence rebellion breaks out
	1948	France crushes the rebellion with the loss of 80,000 lives
0–1959	**1958**	Madagascar gains internal self-government
0–1969	**1960**	**Jun. 26** Madagascar becomes independent as the Malagasy Republic: Philibert Tsiranana is the first president
	1965	Tsiranana is re-elected president
0–1979	**1972**	Mass demonstrations force Tsiranana to resign: the army takes power under Gen. Gabriel Ramanantsoa
	1975	President Didier Ratsiraka nationalizes foreign-owned business and changes the country's name to Madagascar
0–1989	**1982**	Ratsiraka is re-elected president
	1983	Ratsiraka introduces measures to liberalize the economy
0–1999	**1991**	President Ratsiraka places Albert Zafy in control of a transitional government
	1992	A multiparty constitution is approved after a referendum
	1993	Zafy is elected president
	1996	Zafy resigns from the presidency after impeachment by the National Assembly
	1997	Ratsiraka returns to power after presidential elections
0–	**2000**	Tropical storms and floods cause great damage
	2002	Marc Ravalomanana becomes president when Ratsiraka accepts electoral defeat and leaves country

Queen Ranavalona I
She succeeded to the throne upon the death of her husband, Radama I, in 1828.

Franco–Merina War
The Merina were again defeated by the French forces in 1895.

Queen Ranavalona III
French troops deposed the last monarch of Madagsar from her throne in 1897.

© DIAGRAM

Mauritius

In 1722, French colonists from Réunion settled on Mauritius, which t[...] called the Île de France. They used slave labor to develop the land. In[...] 1810, the British occupied the island. They called it Mauritius, the na[...] used by the Dutch who controlled the island between 1598 and 1710. The British abolished slavery in 1833. Sugar became the main crop a[...] more than 450,000 laborers were imported from India between 1835[...] 1907. Mauritius became independent on March 12, 1968. The British monarch, represented by a governor-general, was its head of state.

From 1968–1982, the Mauritius Labor Party (MLP) led by the prim[...] minister Sir Seewoosagur Ramgoolam ruled the country. Although pr[...] Western, he opposed Britain's transfer of Diego Garcia from Mauriti[...] authority in 1965. Britain leased the island to the US and most of the people of Diego Garcia, called the Ilois, were resettled on Mauritius a[...] Seychelles. Mauritius has claimed the Chagos Archipelago since 198[...] In 2000, the Ilois won a victory when the British High Court ruled tha[...] Britain had acted illegally in expelling them.

In 1982, the left-wing Mauritian Militant Movement (MMM) won control of the government and Anerood Jugnauth became prime mini[...] In 1983, Jugnauth formed the Militant Socialist Movement (MSM) a[...] an alliance with two other parties, which won further elections in 198[...] In 1992, Mauritius became a republic. Sir Cassam Uteem became president, though the prime minister remained head of the governmen[...] In 1995, Sir Navinchandra Ramgoolam, the MLP leader, became prim[...] minister. However, following elections in 2000, Jugnauth returned as prime minister.

Sir Seewoosagur Ramgoolam
He became prime minister of Mauritius after the island won independence in 1968.

Sir Anerood Jugnauth
He became prime minister when the MMM won control of the island in 1982.

Mauritius timeline		
	1715 CE	The French claim the island and name it Île de France
19th century		
	1810	The British capture the island and rename it Mauritius
1950–1959	**1957**	Mauritius gains internal self-government
1960–1969	**1968 Mar. 12**	Mauritius becomes independent with Sir Seewoos[...] Ramgoolam as prime minister
1980–1989	**1982**	The Militant Mauritian Movement (MMM) wins elections and[...] AneroodJugnauth becomes prime minister
1990–1999	**1992**	Mauritius becomes a republic
	1995	Sir Navinchandra Ramgoolam replaces Jugnauth as prime[...] minister
2000–	**2000**	Jugnauth returns as prime minister

o Tomé and Príncipe

960, a group of nationalists, including Manuel Pinto Da Costa and
uel Trovoada, set up the Movement for the Liberation of São Tomé
Príncipe (MLSTP). They were unable to operate on the islands
ch were then governed as a Portuguese overseas province. Their
n base from 1961 was in Gabon. After a military regime seized
er in Portugal in April 1974, it granted self-government to the
ids. Full independence was achieved on July 12, 1975. The first
ident was Da Costa, while Trovoada became prime minister. Most of
Portuguese settlers left the islands, depriving it of much of its skilled
onnel. The new government followed socialist policies. It
onalized the plantations and took control of retail businesses, though
ate property and investment were still permitted. The MLSTP
me the sole legal party and the government set up a secret police
e to maintain control. However, the country remained unaligned in
ign affairs, but continued good relations with Portugal.
the 1970s, Da Costa brought charges against Trovoada who was
nissed in 1979 and jailed for two years. In 1988, with the economy in
line, Da Costa accepted tough economic reforms imposed by the
rnational Monetary Fund (IMF). A constitution introduced in 1990
to the first multiparty elections in 1991. Trovoada stood as leader of
Democratic Convergence, a party founded in 1987, and was
orious after Da Costa withdrew. He continued the economic reforms
abolished the secret police. In 1995, the government granted self rule
ríncipe. Following an attempted coup in 1995, Trovoada was
ected in 1996 but, in 2001, Fradique de Menezes became president.

Manuel Pinto da Costa
He became president in
July 1975 and served in
this role until 1990.

Miguel Trovoada
He became president after
the first multiparty election
since independence.

o Tomé and Príncipe timeline		
e-19th century		
	1470 CE	The Portuguese discover the islands of São Tomé and Príncipe
	1522	The Portuguese crown takes over Sào Tomé and Príncipe
:h century		
	1875	Slave labor is officially abolished
50–1959	**1953**	The Batepa massacre: troops kill hundreds of plantation workers who are on strike
50–1969	**1960**	The Committee for the Liberation of São Tomé and Príncipe is formed
70–1979	**1975 July 12**	São Tomé and Príncipe become independent: Manuel Pinto da Costa becomes president
90–1999	**1990**	Da Costa resigns. Miguel Trovoada becomes president after the first multiparty presidential election since independence
	1996	President Miguel Trovoada is reelected president
00–	**2001**	Fradique de Menezes is elected president

© DIAGRAM

Seychelles

Twin celebrations
This stamp was issued in 1976 to mark both the independence of the Seychelles, and the bicentenary of United States' independence.

In 1742, the French rulers of what is now Mauritius sent explorers to Seychelles. French colonists arrived in 1770, together with African slaves. They created a supply station for French ships sailing to Asia. they cut down the forests and killed the wildlife, including giant tortoises, greatly damaging the environment. In 1815, France surrende the islands to Britain. The British made the Seychelles a dependency Mauritius, which they had also taken from France. Seychelles became separate colony in 1903. In 1964, two political parties were formed. C was the right-wing Seychelles Democratic Party (SDP), which oppose independence. It was led by James Mancham. The other was the socia Seychelles People's United Party (SPUP), led by France-Albert René, The SDP won the 1970 elections and Mancham became prime minist The Seychelles became an independent republic on June 29, 1976.

The first president, James Mancham, appointed René as his prime minister. But Mancham was deposed in a bloodless coup in 1977; Rer became president. He suspended the constitution, dissolved the nation assembly and introduced moderate socialist policies. In 1979, fearing that he, too, might be deposed by a coup, René made his Seychelles People's Progressive Front (SPPF) the country's sole legal party. He survived several unsuccessful coups. In 1979, 1984, and 1991, René the only candidate in the presidential elections, but, under pressure fro aid donors and others, his government legalized other parties. Manch returned home in 1993 to stand as opposition candidate in multiparty elections. But René was reelected in 1993, 1998 and 2001. Under Rer the country's economy developed quickly. Tourism has become the country's leading source of income.

James Mancham
He was the first leader of the Seychelles Democratic Party (SDP) in 1964, and became prime minister in 1970.

Seychelles timeline		
	1756 CE	France claims the Seychelles
	1794	The British occupy the Seychelles
19th century	**1814**	France formally cedes the Seychelles to Britain
1970–1979	**1976**	**Jun. 29** The Seychelles become independent: James Mancham is the first president
	1977	France Albert René becomes president after a military cou
	1979	René's Marxist Seychelles People's Progressive Front (SPF becomes the only legal party
1980–1989	**1981**	A coup attempt by foreign mercenaries is defeated
1990–1999	**1991**	Opposition parties are legalized and Marxism is abandone
	1993	René defeats Mancham in the first multi-party presidential elections
	1998	René and the SPPF are again reelected
2000–	**2001**	René is again reelected president

bo, A. E., et al. *The Making of Modern
ica*, New York: Longman (1986)

old, Guy, *Political and Economic
cyclopedia of Africa*, Detroit: Gale,
93)

old, Guy, *Wars in the Third World since
45,* London: Cassell (1995)

old, Guy, *Historical Dictionary of Civil
rs in Africa*, New York: Scarecrow Press
99)

old, Guy, *Guide to African Political and
onomic Development*, London: Fitzroy
arborn (2001)

nte, Molefe, *The Afrocentric Idea,*
iladelphia: Temple University Press
87)

raclough, G., ed. *Hammond Concise
las of World History.* Union, N.J.:
mmond (2001)

ly, C.A., *Atlas of the British Empire*, New
rk: Facts On File (1989)

, Morag, *Contemporary Africa*, New York:
ngman (1986)

in, Robert, *Art and Society in Africa,* New
rk: Longman (1980)

azan, Naomi, et al. *Politics and Society in
ontemporary Africa*, Boulder, Colo.: Lynne
enner (1992)

lier's Encyclopedia. New York: Collier's
997)

ok, Chris, and Stevenson, J., *World
story Since 1914*, London: Longman
991)

rtin, Philip D., et al., eds. *African History*,
ew York: Longman (1995)

Davidson, Basil, *Discovering Africa's Past*,
London: Longman (1978)

Diagram Group, *African History On File,* New
York: Facts On File (2003)

Diagram Group, *Encyclopedia of African
Nations,* New York: Facts On File (2002)

Diagram Group, *Encyclopedia of African
Peoples,* New York: Facts On File (2000)

Diagram Group, *Nations of Africa,* New York:
Facts On File (1997)

Diagram Group, *Peoples of Central Africa,*
New York: Facts On File (1997)

Diagram Group, *Peoples of East Africa,* New
York: Facts On File (1997)

Diagram Group, *Peoples of North Africa,*
New York: Facts On File (1997)

Diagram Group, *Peoples of Southern Africa,*
New York: Facts On File (1997)

Diagram Group, *Peoples of West Africa,* New
York: Facts On File (1997)

Diagram Group, *Religions On File,* New York:
Facts On File (1990)

Diagram Group, *Timelines On File, 4 vols.*
New York: Facts On File (2000)

Diop, C. A., *The African Origin of Civilization:
Myth or Reality*, New York: Lawrence Hill
(1974)

Ehret, Christopher, *Southern Nilotic History*,
Evanston, Ill.: Northwestern University Press
(1971)

Encyclopedia Britannica, Chicago:
Encyclopedia Britannica, 2000.

Europa World Yearbook 2002, 2 vols.
London: Europa Publications (2002)

©DIAGRAM

Bibliography

Freeman-Grenville, G.S.P., *The New Atlas of African History*, New York: Simon & Schuster (1999)

Gailey, Harry A., *History of Africa*, Malabar, Fla.: Krieger (1999)

Gaisford, John, ed. *Atlas of Man*, New York: St. Martin's Press (1978)

Garlake, Peter, *Kingdoms of Africa*, New York: Peter Bedrick Books (1990)

General History of Africa, 8. vols. Berkeley, CA: University of California Press (1990–99)

Gordon, A. A., and Gordon, D. L., eds. *Understanding Contemporary Africa*, Boulder, Colo.: Lynne Rienner (1992)

Hammond, Dorothy, and Jablow, Alta, *The Africa That Never Was*, Prospect Heights, Ill.: Waveland Press (1992)

Hargreaves, John D., *Decolonization of Africa*, New York: Longman (1983)

July, Robert W., *A History of the African People*, Prospect Heights, Ill.: Waveland Press (1992)

Kinder, Herman, and Hilgemann, Werner, *The Penguin Atlas of World History*, 2 vols. London: Penguin (1980)

Loftus, Ernest, *A Visual History of Africa*, London: Evans (1976)

McEvedy, Colin, *The Penguin Atlas of African History,* New York: Penguin (1995)

Northrup, David, *Africa's Discovery of Europe*, New York: Oxford University Press (2002)

O'Connor, Anthony, *The African City*, New York: Africana (1983)

Oliver, Roland, *The African Experience*, London: Weidenfeld and Nicolson (1991

Oliver, Roland, and Atmore, Anthony, *Afric Since 1800*, New York: Cambridge University Press (1994)

Oliver, Roland, and Fage, J.D., *A Short History of Africa*, London: Penguin (1990

Olson, James S., *Peoples of Africa,* Westport, Conn.: Greenwood (1996)

Page, Willie F., *Encyclopedia of African History and Culture*, 3 vols. New York: Fa On File (2002)

Sibanda, M., Moyana, H. and Gumbo, S.[*The African Heritage,* Harare: Zimbabwe Educational Books (1986)

Stewart, John, *African States and Rulers*, Jefferson, N.C.: McFarland (1994)

Tordoff, William, *Government and Politics Africa*, Bloomington: Indiana University Press (1993)

UNESCO, *General History of Africa,* 8 vols Berkeley, CA.: University of California Pre (1981–1992)

Wepman, Dennis, *Africa: The Struggle for Independence,* New York: Facts On File (1993)

Willett, Frank, *African Art*, New York: Tham & Hudson (1993)

World Book Encyclopedia, Chicago: Worl Book (2002)

Zell, Hans M., Bundy, Carol and Coulon, Virginia, *A New Reader's Guide to Africar Literature,* New York: Africana (1983)

cha, Sanni 72
oud, Ibrahim 84
 al-Krim 65
bakar, Abdulsalam 73
eampong, Ignatius 42
ommani, king of the
nboukou 49
wa, Battle of 37
verki, Issias 34
can National Congress
 82, 96
djo, Ahmadou 18
nadu, Sultan 71
S 12, 82, 94
ffo, Frederick 42
eçiras conference (1906)

eria 6–7
Muhammad 31
erican Colonization
ciety 54
n, Idi 88, 94
nola 8–9
rah, Joseph 42
bic language 6, 62, 84
ame, Jean-Hilaire 38

gaza, Jean-Baptiste 16
ewa, Sir Abubakar Tafawa

nda, Hastings 58
3ashir, Omar 84
dié, Henri Konan 48
gin, Menachim 30
gium and Belgian rule 16,
 , 74
n Ali, Zine al Abidine 92

Ben Bella, Muhammad
 Ahmad 6
Bendjedid, Chadli 6
Benin 10–11
Biafra 72–3
Biya, Paul 18
Boganda, Barthélémy 20
Bokassa, Jean Bédel 20–1
Bongo, El Hadj Omar 38
Borgnis-Desbordes, Colonel
 71
Botswana 12–13
Boumédienne, Houari 6
Bourguiba, Habib 92
Bouteflika, Abdelaziz 6
de Brazza, Pierre de
 Savorgnan 27
Britain and British rule 12,
 18, 30, 34, 40, 42, 50, 52,
 58, 72, 78, 80, 82, 86, 94,
 96, 98, 104, 106
Burkina Faso 14–15, 90
Burundi 16–17, 24
Busia, Kofi 42
Buyoya, Pierre 16

C

Cabral, Amilcar 46
Cabral, Luiz 46
Cameroon 18–19
Cape Verde 100
Caprivi Strip 68
Carthage 93
Central African Federation
 96, 98
Central African Republic
 20–1
Chad 22–3
Chilembwe, John 58

Chiluba, Frederick 96
Chissano, Joaquim 66
Comoros 101
Compaoré, Blaise 14, 90
Congo, Democratic Republic
 of 24–5, 68, 74
Congo, Republic of 25–6
Conté, Lansana 44
Côte d'Ivoire see Ivory Coast
Coulibaly, Quezzin 15

D

Da Costa, Manuel Pinto 105
Dacko, David 20
Dahomey 91; see also Benin
Déby, Idriss 22
Denard, Bob 101
Dhlakama, Afonso 66
Dia, Mamadou 76
Diori, Hamani 70
Diouf, Abdou 76
Djibouti 28–9
Doe, Samuel 54
dos Santos, José Eduardo 8

E

Economic Community of
 West African States 54
Egal, Mohamed Ibrahim 80
Egypt 30–1
Equatorial Guinea 32–3
Eritrea 34–5
Ethiopia 34, 36–7
Eyadéma, Gnassingbe 90

F

Farouk I of Egypt 30
Firestone Tire and Rubber
 Company 54

Index

FLN (Algerian National Liberation Front) 6
Fourah Bay College 79
France and French rule 6, 10, 14, 18, 20, 22, 26, 28, 30, 38, 44, 48, 60, 62, 70, 76–7, 90, 92, 101–2
Franco, Francisco 33
FRELIMO (Front for the Liberation of Mozambique) 66
Fulani states 47

G

Gabon 38–9
Gambia 40–1
Garang, John 84
De Gaulle, Charles 63
Gbagbo, Laurent 48
George VI 53
Germany and German rule 16, 18, 57, 68–9, 74, 77, 88, 90
Ghana 42–3, 90–1
Gouled, Aptidon Hassan 28
Gowon, General 72
Great Trek, the 83
Great Zimbabwe 99
Grunitzky, Nicolas 90
Guei, Robert 48
Guelleh, Ismail Omar 28
Guinea 44–5
Guinea-Bissau 46–7

H

Habré, Hissène 22
Habyarimana, Juvénal 74
Haidalla, Mohammed Khouna 62

Haile Selassie I 36
Hassan II of Morocco 62, 64
HIV see AIDS
Houphouët-Boigny, Félix 48–9
Hutu people 16, 24, 74–5

I

Ialá, Kumba 46
Idris I of Libya 56
International Court of Justice 22, 68
International Monetary Fund 14, 66, 105
Israel 30
Italy and Italian rule 34, 36, 56–7, 80
Ivory Coast 48–9

J

Jammeh, Yahya 40
Jawara, Sir Dawda 40
Jonathan, Chief 52
Jugnauth, Sir Aneerood 104

K

Kabbah, Ahmad Tejan 78
Kabila, Joseph 24–5
Kagame, Paul 74
Kariba Dam 96
Kasavubu, Joseph 25
Katanga 24
Kaunda, Kenneth 96
Kayibanda, Grégoire 74
Keita, Modibo 60
Kenya 50–1
Kenyatta, Jomo 50
Kenyatta, Margaret Wambui 50

Kérékou, Mathieu 10
Khama, Sir Seretse 12
de Klerk, Frederik Willem
Kolingba, André 20
Konaré, Alpha Oumar 60
Kountché, Seyni 70
Kufuor, John Agyekum 42
Kutako, Hosea 68

L

Lamizana, Sangoulé 14
League of Nations 16, 18, 68, 74, 82, 90
Lekhanya, Justin 52
Leopold II of Belgium 25
Lesotho 12, 52–3
Letsie III of Lesotho 52
Liberia 54–5
Libya 22, 56–7
Lissouba, Pascal 26
Livingstone, David 13
Lumumba, Patrice 24

M

Machel, Samora 66
Macías Nguema, Francisco 32
Madagascar 102–3
Maga, Hubert 10
al-Mahdi, Sadiq 84
Mainassara, Ibrahim 70
Makoko, king of the Bateke 27Malawi 58–9
Mali 60–1, 76
Malloum, Félix 22
Mamadou, Tandja 70
Mancham, James 106
Mandela, Nelson 82
Mane, Ansumane 46

jai, Albert 78
jai, Sir Milton 78–9
ire, Ketumile 12
samba-Débat, Alphonse

Mau 50–1
ritania 62–4
ritius 104
a, Léon 38
ki, Thabo 82
da, André-Marie 18
racen, the 7
elik II of Ethiopia 37
ezes, Fradique de 105
gistu, Haile-Mariam 34,

mbero, Michel 16
pa, Benjamin 88
utu Sese-Seko 24
jae, Festus 12
gho naba 15
, Daniel arap 50
hehle, Ntsu 52
noh, Joseph 78
teiro, António 100
occo 62, 64–5
hoeshoe I of the Basotho
–3
hoeshoe II of the
sotho 52
isili, Bethuel 52
ambique 66–7MPLA
pular Movement for the
dependence of Angola)
9
vati I of Swaziland 86
vati III of Swaziland 86
arak, Hosni 30
jabe, Robert 98

Muhammad V of Morocco 64
Muhammad VI of Morocco
 64
Muluzi, Bakili 58
Museveni, Yoweri 74, 94
Mutesa I of Buganda 95
Mutesa II of Buganda 94
Mwambutsa IV of Burundi
 16–17
Mwanawasa, Levy 96
Mwinyi, Ali Hassan 88

N
Namibia 68–9, 82
Napoleon 31
Narrimari, queen of Egypt 30
an-Nasser, Gamal Abd 30
Ndadaye, Melchior 16
Neguib, Muhammad 30
Neto, Antonio Agostinho 8
Ngouabi, Marien 26
Niger 70–1
Nigeria 18, 72–3
Nimeiri, Gaafar Muhammad
 84
Njoya, king of the Bamum 19
Nkomo, Joshua 98
Nkrumah, Kwame 42
Nkumbula, Harry 96
Ntare V of Burundi 16
Ntaryamira, President 74
Ntibantungana, President 16
Nujoma, Sam 68
Nyerere, Julius 88

O
Oba Ovonramwen 11
Obasanjo, Olesegun 72
Obiang Nguema, Teodoro 32

Obote, Milton 74, 94
Ojukwu, Colonel 72
Olympio, Sylvanus 90
Omdurman, Battle of 85
Organization of African Unity
 64
Osman, Aden Abdullah 80
Oueddei, Goukoun 22
Ouédraogo, Jean-Baptiste
 14
Ould Daddah, Moktar 62–3
Ousmane, Mahamane 70

P
Patassé, Ange-Félix 20
Pereira, Aristide 100
Pires, Pedro 100
Polisario front 62, 64
Portugal and Portuguese rule
 8, 46, 66, 100, 105
Principe 105

Q
al-Quaddafi, Muammar 56

R
Rabib bin Fadl Allah 23
Ramanantsoa, Gabriel 102
Ramgoolam, Sir
 Seewoosagur 104
Ranavalona I, queen of
 Madagascar 103
Ranavalona III, queen of
 Madagascar 103
Ratsimandrava, Richard 102
Ratsiraka, Didier 102
Ravalomanana, Marc 102
Rawlings, Jerry 42
RENAMO (Mozambique

Index

National Resistance Movement) 66
René, France-Albert 106
Rhodes, Cecil 99
Rhodesia 96, 98; *see also* Zimbabwe
Roberts, Joseph Jenkins 55
Rwanda 16–17, 24, 74–5

S

al-Sadat, Muhammad Anwar 30–1
es Sadek, Muhammad 93
Saibou, Ali 70
Samori Touré 71
Sankara, Thomas 14
Sankoh, Foday 78
São Tomè and Principe 105
Sassou-Nguesso, Denis 26
Savimbi, Jonas 8
Sawyer, Amos 54
Schweitzer, Albert 39
Senegal 76–7
Senghor, Léopold 76
Seychelles 106
Sharpeville massacre 82
Shermarke, Abder-Rashid 80
Siad Barre, Muhammad 80
Sierra Leone 78–9
slavery 47, 104
Smith, Ian 98
Sobhuza II of Swaziland 86–7
Soglo, Christophe 10
Soglo, Nicéphore 10

Soilih, Ali 101
Somalia 80–1
South Africa 12, 66, 68, 82–3
Spain and Spanish rule 32, 64–5
Speke, John Hanning 95
Stevens, Siaka 78
Strasser, Valentine 78
Sudan 84–5
Suez crisis (1956) 30
SWAPO (South West African People's Organization) 68–9
Swaziland 86–7

T

Tanzania 88–9
Taya, Maaouiya Ould Sidi Ahmed 62
Togo 90–1
Toivo, Animba Herman 68
Tolbert, William 54
Tombalbaye, Ngarta 22
Toure, Ahmadou 60
Touré, Sékou 44
Traoré, Moussa 60
Trovoada, Miguel 105
Ts'akha Maryam 35
Tsiranana, Philibert 102
Tubman, William 54
Tunisia 92–3
Tutsi people 16, 24, 74–5

U

Uganda 24, 94–5
UNITA (National Union for the Total Liberation of Angola) 8–9, 90
United Nations 18, 34, 56, 64, 68, 80
United States 56
Uteem, Sir Cassam 104

V

Vieira, Joåo 46
Vittorio Emanuele III 81

W

Wade, Abdoulaye 76
Wanké, Daouda 70
Western Sahara 62, 64
Williams, Ruth 12
World War I 68, 90

Y

Yaméogo, Maurice 14
Yhombi-Opango, Joachim 26
Yom Kippur War 30
Youlou, Fulbert 26

Z

Zafy, Albert 102
Zaïre *see* Congo, Democratic Republic of
Zambia 58, 96–7
ZANU, ZAPU and ZANU- 66, 98
Zenawi, Meles 36
Zerbo, Sayé 14
Zimbabwe 58, 98–9